RHYME AND REST

RHYME AND REST

Poetic Devotions for Weary Pilgrims

KERRIE DEBERRY

Illustrations by Megan York

RESOURCE *Publications* · Eugene, Oregon

RHYME AND REST
Poetic Devotions for Weary Pilgrims

Resource Publications
An Imprint of Wipf and Stock Publishers
199 W. 8th Ave., Suite 3
Eugene, OR 97401

www.wipfandstock.com

PAPERBACK ISBN: 979-8-3852-0521-9
HARDCOVER ISBN: 979-8-3852-0522-6
EBOOK ISBN: 979-8-3852-0523-3

05/21/24

To Justin. Thank you for being my friend, encouraging me to write this book, reading it over, giving your input, and loving me with courage, conviction, gentleness, and playfulness. You make me laugh and help me take myself less seriously. I love life with you.

Contents

Acknowledgements

There are so many people who were used by the Lord to bring this project to life. I want to honor and thank a few of them.

To my dad and mom, Robert and Joan Kiley. You have always been a steadfast presence and influence in my life, you are a place I feel safe. Thank you for encouraging me that I was capable, even when I doubted it. For helping me see what is truly important, i.e. not crying over spilled milk. Dad, for singing funny lines outside our bedrooms with your guitar when we didn't want to get up. It didn't always get me out of bed, but I loved it. My love of rhyme and song began with you. I love you both dearly.

Thank you to my grandmother, Florence Kiley, who I have so many memories of spending time with over a cup of tea. She never published her lovely rhyming children's book, but I hope to keep her legacy of love for God and poetry alive. I miss her soft and gentle spirit.

Thank you to many others who have discipled and mentored me over the years. Kathy Lambros, for all the Bible studies, cards, letters, encouragement, and friendship, you continue to be a gift from God. Sony Thayer, thank you for being my dear friend. Thank you for loving me before you even knew me, when you heard we were having our fourth daughter, for praying, and for being a constant encourager to me as a mother, a wife, and a writer. Doug and Delora Sims, how would I have tackled so much editing and writing if you didn't offer to take our girls almost every Friday for over a year? Your gift of time and love is immeasurable. Rondi Lauterbach, thank you for shepherding me during seminary with Justin and loving me from afar while we worked through the early years in ministry.

Thank you to those who were part of the writing process. Bethany Reinhold, for almost seventeen years of friendship you have sharpened me theologically and inspired so much of the poetry in this book. Thank you for pointing out where God was at work when I didn't see it. Amy Oneil, I'll always remember our long walk down the road in Pheonix where you gave me the idea of a fifty-two-week devotional. Thank you for your encouragement in this process. Carleigh Foland, for being an incredible encourager and friend. Your words of specific affirmation have been a balm to my soul in moments when I was tempted to give up.

Megan York, thank you for being such a joy to work with as an illustrator. I so admire your gifts, integrity, and work ethic. Thank you for tackling this with me in such a gracious, professional way.

Thank you to the many friends who took a moment to ask me, "When are you going to publish your book, Kerrie?" At some point I had to start taking that more seriously—maybe this is from the Lord? Thank you for verbalizing your encouragement.

Thank you, Piper, Reagan, Greta, and Finley. Thank you for letting Mommy escape and write when I needed to. You have given me so much grace, especially when I refused to open the door to the reading room, or "made you" watch Little House on the Prairie while I worked. I love you with all my heart, my little women. God blessed me beyond what I could have imagined in letting Daddy and I have you for a little while this side of heaven.

I'm so grateful for my years alongside Justin at Westminster Seminary California. The theology, the wisdom, and the community of friends have blessed us richly.

Lastly, I'm thankful for my church home in Madison, West Center Baptist. It's beautiful to see the wisdom of God in giving us a community to learn, grow, fail, and hear the good news again and again.

Introduction

THE TRAJECTORY OF MY LIFE changed in college. Unexpectedly and sovereignly, between playing soccer, studying, and partying, the Holy Spirit gave me a new heart one night in Easton, Pennsylvania. Jesus became real to me, I received him for what he truly is, Lord and Savior. My desires began to change, but so did my mind. I was hungry to learn the beauties and truths of the gospel with an intellectual curiosity I had never experienced before. It was like my deepest thirst had been quenched, but then suddenly I was given an unquenchable thirst for the things of God. I remember sitting down in a coffee shop the week I became a Christian to read R.C. Sproul's *The Holiness of God*. I finished it in one sitting. That season began a growing love for reading and writing in general, but especially for reading and writing about God's grace in Christ.

Fast forward ten years. I'm married and my hands are full with two babies, dirty diapers, car seats (I don't think the shoulder tightness has fully gone away), meals, work, family, friends, and church life. Justin (my husband) was progressing in his banking career and one day came home to tell me he was sensing a call to become a pastor. Not a big surprise as he was already acting like one. After a lot of counsel and prayer, we moved from Tucson, AZ, to San Diego, CA, for three years of seminary at Westminster Seminary, CA. And we *firmly decided*, "No more babies until after seminary!" I proceeded to get pregnant twice in two years (yes, we know how that works). With four little ones under five, I suddenly found myself in a new place (South Dakota . . . what?) and in a new role as a wife to a pastor. BTW, I like that better than "pastor's wife." In the midst of all that, when a rare, glorious moment of peace came at the end of the day, I would write. For me, writing is worship. It is lament, joy, confession, and supplication from my brain through my heart onto the page. The poems in this book are the product of those moments. Initially, they were simply a way to commune with God and not talk Justin's ear off.

Then I began to discover a deeper joy in writing, mainly in weaving theology into the tapestry of each poem. As I live through my own trials and walk with others through theirs, it has become a way for me to express joy and sadness, victory and loss, hope and hurt, pleasure and pain. These are personal psalms. And like the Psalms, I hope they are universally relevant. I hope they are evergreen in the lives of all those walking through a good but fallen world. I hope they lead you away from discouragement, away from yourself, and toward the Savior.

I realize poetry is a unique style of writing and perhaps not everyone's cup of tea. My prayer is that even if you prefer straight-shooting prose or well-told stories, you might take a sip. God invented poetry (the Bible is filled with it) to communicate truth in a way that engages our imagination. It is a medium of beauty, vulnerability, and terseness. The format of fifty-two weeks is intentional. I love daily devotionals. We have a few of our favorites on the living room bookshelf. But the thought of giving you a week to ruminate on one topic sounded really good. Slowing down, going deeper, pondering, staying, praying, is what I hope to assist in. It's easy to rush through life. It's easy to rush God. It's hard to be slow, a discipline really. I don't have to tell you there are a thousand and one things *demanding* your attention at this very moment. Yet this is where I believe God loves to feed our souls. Not mainly in a Bible drive-thru, but a nourishing home cooked meal we take time to savor. You can only taste and see that the Lord is good if you take time to taste and see.

Warning: there may be a few gut punches in the pages that follow, for which I'm sorry/not sorry. Remember God's heart, he wounds so he can bind up. He brings light so he can clean up. He makes low so he can build up. My heart is to challenge you the way I need God to challenge me—humbling me with godly grief that produces a repentance that leads to salvation without regret.

The format of each week is: ponder, stay, and pray. The ponder questions invite you to reflect on God as he has revealed himself in Scripture, expressed in that week's poem. The stay questions push you to apply the theology and themes to real life. The pray section draws you to related Scriptures for personal meditation and prayer. I want to help cultivate the wonderful practice of praying Scripture.

Enjoy this book as a personal devotional. Enjoy it as a small group study. Keep it on your nursery table when you are up at 2am feeding the baby. Keep it in your grandma book box to read with the grandkids.

Thank you with all my heart for opening yourself up to these words. May you be blessed; and may you be transformed by the renewal of your mind, that by testing you may discern what is the will of God, what is good and acceptable and perfect (Rom 12:2).

1. THE NEW YEAR

Dear parenting friend,
starting a fresh new year.
Whether a new job, new school,
or empty nesting with a tear.
Sending your kids to school,
homeschooling for the first time.
Learning how to juggle a job,
running a home with barely time to unwind.
Entering a brand new season,
perhaps a new baby on the way.
Wherever you are in your calling,
I hope you find encouragement today.
Making lunches, cleaning clothes,
working in or out of the home.
Working through a difficult marriage,
or generally just feeling alone.
You have a faithful Savior,
who knows all of your fears.
He's walked this road before you,
shedding his own salty tears.
So when your fears assault you,
and anxiety strikes its ugly head.
You run to God's promises and choose,
to trust in them instead.
Unknowns and what ifs have no place,
we leave tomorrow's worries out of today.
Sufficient for the day is its own trouble,
in Matthew 6:34 our Lord did say.
Remember that the biggest thief of joy,
is to compare to others around you.
Live before the face of God,
and stay the course he is calling you to.
Faithfulness, not perfection,
consistency, not all over the place.
Humility to say, I need help,
I messed up, or I need more grace.

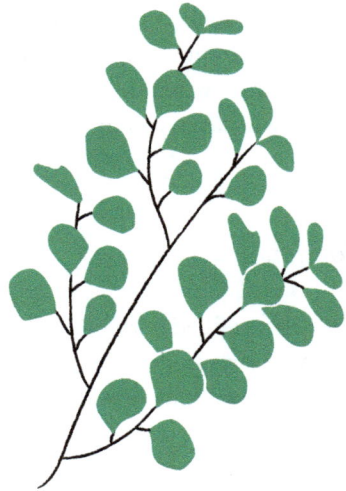

Moving towards others not away,
seeking their good above mine.
Getting outside ourselves,
can really do wonders divine.
Seeing our spouse as an ally,
cultivating our friendship and making sure to laugh.
Representing Jesus to our kids,
and giving them time and a half.
Resting my friends, instead of fretting,
for in Jesus' righteousness you are safe and free.
For in him you are known, loved, forgiven, redeemed,
your cares and worries he can surely carry.
So go confidently into this year,
knowing the one who has set affection on you.
He is faithful when we are not,
and he will carry you through.

Ponder

The Bible is filled with examples of the new or unknown provoking fear in human hearts—Abraham and Abimelech; the spies sent into the promised land; Peter walking on water. While not all fear is bad, there is often an idol lurking underneath it (comfort, power, control, approval, etc.) Spend some time thinking on the relationship between change, fear, and idols.

Stay

When life is changing, one of greatest helps to spiritual health and mental sanity is keeping the main things the main thing. Take time this week to write down the top five to ten most important callings in your life. Begin with relationship with God.

Pray

Micah 6:8: "He has told you, O man, what is good; and what does the LORD require of you but to do justice, and to love kindness, and to walk humbly with your God?"

Psalm 37:27–28, 30: "Turn away from evil and do good; so shall you dwell forever. For the LORD loves justice; he will not forsake his saints . . . The mouth of the righteous utters wisdom, and his tongue speaks justice. The law of his God is in his heart; his steps do not slip."

Titus 2:11–13: "For the grace of God has appeared, bringing salvation for all people, training us to renounce ungodliness and worldly passions, and to live self-controlled, upright, and godly lives in the present age, waiting for our blessed hope, the appearing of the glory of our great God and Savior Jesus Christ . . . "

2. WHEN I'M OLD AND GRAY

One day when I'm old and gray,
and the years have flown by.
I'll look around & miss the sounds,
the laughing as they run by.
I'll miss stepping on the Legos,
crunching Cheerios under my feet.
I'll miss them learning how to read,
and their little voices oh so sweet.
I'll miss their hugs and kisses,
their snuggling on my lap.
Their cute little conversations,
and showing me how they tap.
Some things I will not miss,
like boogies, whining and fights.
Cleaning pee off the carpet,
or throw ups in the middle of night.
I know when I am pining,
to get this and to get that done.
And someone comes in crying,
or all my clean up gets undone.
The temptation to grow angry,
resentful and forlorn.
Towards my little children,
can creep in like a storm.
For all the interruptions,
that enter in my days.
I have two choices I can choose,
to fight or to embrace.
God knows the things I need to do,
he knows what must get done.
But working on my sinful heart,
is his priority number one.
So today if your littles,
are wreaking havoc on your plans.
Embrace the trouble, love them well,
and trust your loving Father's hand.

For this momentary work,
is storing up for you.
Sweet treasures of eternity,
that Christ has won for you.
As you run to him,
his Spirit please implore.
For he will help you if you ask,
and give you grace so you'll endure.
Love those whom God gave you,
squeeze and hold them tight.
Embrace the interruptions,
they may be what you need tonight.

Ponder

There is a planned and spontaneous aspect to every day and every season of life. Does planning or spontaneity come more naturally to you? Meditate on the truth that God works through both.

Stay

How would your life change if you believed every interruption was a divine appointment? Take some time and ask the Lord's forgiveness for any unbelief in your heart when the day or season is interrupted. Then pray for help to see him as the One behind every disturbance and intrusion.

Pray

Proverbs 19:21: "Many are the plans in the mind of a man, but it is the purpose of the LORD that will stand."

Job 42:2: "I know that you can do all things, and that no purpose of yours can be thwarted."

Mark 5: 27–34: "She had heard the reports about Jesus and came up behind him in the crowd and touched his garment. For she said, "If I touch even his garments, I will be made well." And immediately the flow of blood dried up, and she felt in her body that she was healed of her disease. And Jesus, perceiving in himself that power had gone out from him, immediately turned about in the crowd and said, "Who touched my garments?" And his disciples said to him, "You see the crowd pressing around you, and yet you say, 'Who touched me?'" And he looked around to see who had done it. But the woman, knowing what had happened to her, came in fear and trembling and fell down before him and told him the whole truth. And he said to her, "Daughter, your faith has made you well; go in peace, and be healed of your disease."

3. THE DOUBLE WHISPER

"You failed again," the sound repeats,
an echo in your ear.
"How could you do this again?"
You hear the whisper closing near.
You yelled, you grew impatient,
lost your temper, failed today.
You grasped for control in your hand,
and when it slipped your wrath gave way.
You lusted, you stole, you envied,
you created strife, you gossiped, you stole.
You coveted, you were greedy,
an act of service you did withhold.
Whatever temptation you gave into,
the one you knew you shouldn't of.
Felt so good in the moment,
to grasp onto the sin that you love.
And the voice that whispered "Go ahead,"
and enticed and drew you in.
Played on you by bringing guilt,
the minute your flesh did win.
A whisper that lures, then accuses you,
fulfilling your enemy's desire.
He wants to trick your heart,
he's deceptive; he's a liar.
Wanting you to think,
you're a lost cause and you're done.
What's the point of fighting?
clearly holiness hasn't won.
But then a more gracious whisper,
intrudes into the abyss.
Revealing to you objective truth,
in your self-absorption you may miss.
He whispers joy to your sorrow,
he brings healing to your pain.
He reminds you first of who you are,
and everything you have to gain.

You have an advocate with the Father,
Jesus Christ the righteous one.
His blood, it speaks a better word,
for his mediation has begun.
Whoever believes in him,
all condemnation falls away.
The Clearer of the Guilty,
Defender of the Weak has final say.
So when you feel the weight,
of your sin and all your mess.
You must fight to hear the words,
"But God," in which there's rest.
But God, being rich in mercy,
loved you and took your place.
Even when dead in your trespasses,
made you alive in Christ by his grace.
You have been raised, you have been seated,
in the heavenly places above.
So you don't have to succumb to guilt,
because of secret sins you've done.
Yes, repent and turn, you need to,
but don't linger on your debris.
Instead you plead the blood of Christ,
precious enough to cover your iniquity.
Quiet Satan, Hush your voice!
there is no room for accusation.
I am loved, I am redeemed,
In Jesus Christ . . . I'm a new creation.

Ponder

Think about how Satan is pro-sin on the front side of temptation, and anti-sin on the back side. He is both tempter and accuser. Allow that knowledge empower you against his schemes.

Stay

How does the life, death, and resurrection of Jesus empower you to resist temptation? How does it empower you to fight condemnation after you've sinned? Pray about one specific area of temptation this week.

Pray

1 Corinthians 10:13: "No temptation has overtaken you that is not common to man. God is faithful, and he will not let you be tempted beyond your ability, but with the temptation he will also provide the way of escape, that you may be able to endure it."

Romans 8:1–2: "There is therefore now no condemnation for those who are in Christ Jesus. For the law of the Spirit of life has set you free in Christ Jesus from the law of sin and death."

Zechariah 3:1–2: "Then he showed me Joshua the high priest standing before the angel of the LORD, and Satan standing at his right hand to accuse him. And the LORD said to Satan, 'The Lord rebuke you, O Satan! the LORD who has chosen Jerusalem rebuke you! Is not this a brand plucked from the fire?"

4. LOOK UP

Look up, look up, and see who's there,
look up in front of you.
There are people in your presence,
who need love, touch and smiles too.
And you will savor every moment,
when distraction lies at bay.
You'll be ready, you'll be useful,
to give your time and love away.
Presence with your people,
looking them in the eye.
Not distracted by devices,
and letting moments slip on by.
Our priority are those here,
the ones we can touch and see.
Our family and our neighbors,
our friends in proximity.
Care for them and love them,
ask them questions deep.
Take time to pursue them,
and in true conversation steep.
Our concerns for nation and world,
are good and necessary cares.
But "Go in peace, be warm and filled,"
does not meet our neighbor's need who is right there.
And when we have moments of silence,
or have down-time between tasks.
Instead of scrolling and looking down,
think, pray, seek, and ask:
"Lord, who is it that needs my love?
Who do I need to look up and see?
Who needs an encouragement?
Who needs presence and humanity?
How can I bless when I'm looking down,
instead of looking up into a face?
For the person standing next to me,
is the one I must show grace.

Yes, relationships far away,
are good, and right, and dear.
But not to the neglect and care,
of our loved ones who are near.
For Jesus' incarnation,
was in one place at the set time.
He couldn't be everywhere at once,
nor did he strive for this design.
Limited in his humanity,
face-to-face his mission carried through.
Always walking in the will of the Father,
meant some people he could not pursue.
Faithful to every conversation,
looking up at Zacchaeus in the tree.
The woman at the well,
pouring into his disciples consistently.
Why do we think we can be everywhere,
and carry the weight of people we don't know?
Perhaps our devices have told us this,
our phones taking our hearts where our feet can't go.
A peaceful, quiet, life,
dignified in every way.
Is lived by looking up,
and faithfully working away.
What has God called me to?
Who is physically near to me this week?
This is where I pour my time,
my energy and true fellowship seek.
Look up, look up, and see who's there,
look up in front of you.
There are people in your presence,
who need love, touch, and smiles too.
And you will savor every moment,
when distraction lies at bay.
You'll be ready, you'll be useful,
to give your time and love away.

Ponder

Think about how God is always available and eager to be with you. He is never uninterested in what's on your heart. How does that encourage you, especially when friends and family can often be unavailable or uninterested?

Stay

How often are you spending quality face-to-face time with people in your home, church, and community? How does this compare with time spent on devices?

Pray

Deuteronomy 31:8: "The LORD himself goes before you and will be with you; he will never leave you nor forsake you. Do not be afraid; do not be discouraged."(NIV)

I Thessalonians 3:9–10: "For what thanksgiving can we return to God for you, for all the joy that we feel for your sake before our God, as we pray most earnestly night and day that we may see you face to face . . . "

3 John 1:13–14: "I had much to write to you, but I would rather not write with pen and ink. I hope to see you soon, and we will talk face to face."

5. A LIFE SPENT IN ROMANS 7

When I awake at morning,
and my feet plop on the floor.
I am alerted to the fact,
that the day has much in store.
I truly desire to keep my mind,
my heart and my words today.
Building up, encouraging,
honoring God without delay.
I desire to do what is right,
I delight in the law of God.
But of course it happens surreptitiously,
it feels perplexing and odd.
I don't do the good I want,
instead evil thoughts fill my heart.
And suddenly I'm spiraling down,
far from the place of my morning start.
I see in my members a fight,
and I do what I don't want to do.
Snap at my children and spouse,
selfish thoughts, laziness, to name a few.
My words pierce like an arrow,
my thoughts are far from good.
The thing I just prayed about,
is not going away like I thought it would.
I feel the fight; it feels so strong,
oh wretched woman that I am.
Thank God for Jesus Christ
my Savior, Lord and friend.
The struggle proves he is at work,
he never leaves us all alone.
For the known and unknown sin inside of us,
our best work could not atone.
Who else could deliver us,
from this body of death?
No one but Christ our Savior,
could clean, change, and transform this wretch.

If we didn't experience the fight with sin,
blind and unaware we'd still be.
Unaware of his Holy Spirit's work,
sanctifying our hearts by degree.
For we have died to the law
through Christ's body in order to bear fruit.
The struggles are real and I wrestle with them,
but I am freed by the truth.
And now the commandments that I break,
that formerly proved I was guilty.
Become the ones I delight to do,
because my Savior has first loved me.
Do you feel the battle raging?
Does the weight cause you to fall?
Rest assured if your trust is in Christ,
even on your worst days he's delivered you once for all.
A life walking in the Spirit,
is how you conquer the sin you hate.
How do you walk by the Spirit?
Read ahead to Romans 8.

Ponder

Read Romans 7. Try to read it as a child and write down what strikes you.
How does it give voice to your own battles? How does it give you hope?

Stay

Write down a few areas of sin where God has given you victory through
Jesus Christ our Lord. Not absolute victory (yet), but true victory. Take a
moment to praise God for even small victories each day this week.

Pray

Romans 6:14: "For sin will have no dominion over you, since you are not under law but under grace."

Romans 8:12–15: "So then, brothers, we are debtors, not to the flesh, to live according to the flesh. For if you live according to the flesh you will die, but if by the Spirit you put to death the deeds of the body, you will live. For all who are led by the Spirit of God are sons of God. For you did not receive the spirit of slavery to fall back into fear, but you have received the Spirit of adoption as sons, by whom we cry, 'Abba! Father!.'"

1 Corinthians 15:56–58: "The sting of death is sin, and the power of sin is the law. But thanks be to God, who gives us the victory through our Lord Jesus Christ. Therefore, my beloved brothers, be steadfast, immovable, always abounding in the work of the Lord, knowing that in the Lord your labor is not in vain."

6. OUR FATHER IN HEAVEN

God is my Father, protecting,
leading and strong in his love.
He is intimate, warm, and near me,
yet sovereignly ruling from above.
Therefore, his hand has not slipped,
nor his eyes been taken off any soul.
Every person, every molecule,
he holds all imaginings that we can forebode.

Hallowed Be Your Name

Set apart as holy,
let me bring honor to your name.
By living in times of chaos,
to bring you greater fame.
Perhaps kindness on the tongue,
perhaps gifting space for one to cope.
Refusing to slander, eager to see good,
quick to bring not judgment, but hope.

Your Kingdom Come

Let the citizens of your kingdom,
increasingly reflect your love and grace.
Obey your laws and do good to people,
proclaiming you as trustworthy in our place.
Let Christ reign in our hearts,
as calm, composed dignity we incarnate.
Not overreacting or under-reacting,
but sowing gospel peace that it may this world, saturate.

Your Will Be Done On Earth As It Is In Heaven

Just as the Lord's will in heaven,
is being perfectly carried along.
So Jesus asks us to pray,
as we carry the torch for this song.

God's secret will we do not know,
but his revealed work the Scriptures say.
So let us walk in faith and truth,
and live in obedience this day.
His will is for us to walk with him,
and do what is pleasing in his sight.
Do the dishes, make your plans,
give thanks in everything and do what is right.
For today is what he has given you,
no other day is yours to fret.
For the grace you will need tomorrow morning,
is not today fitted for you just yet.

Give Us This Day Our Daily Bread

God promises he will provide for you,
even when the shelves are empty and bare.
Consider others when you purchase,
and if you buy extra be willing to share.
He who clothes the lilies of the field,
and feeds the sparrow by his command.
Will he not take care of your needs?
Anxiety reveals a heart that does not understand.

And Forgive Us Our Debts

Oh how a trial reveals,
all the sadness and fear in our souls.
None of us worthy to be right with God,
but only the Lamb who has opened the scroll!
Pierced for our transgressions,
crushed for our disbelief.
Access to the Father,
now I can work hard but then peacefully sleep.
If fellowship with God is hindered,
by my response to the world around me.
Then on my knees I pray and cry,
knowing Jesus hears and is gracious to my plea.

As We Also Have Forgiven Our Debtors

Leaving all my anxiety,
at the foot of the cross do I cling.
Forgiving my selfish, angry friend,
for these are the same sins that I bring.
I will not hold against my neighbor,
what I too am guilty of inside.
Instead, I will remember God's mercy,
and how he forgives my deepest pride.

And Lead Us Not Into Temptation

What is your temptation?
Fearing, fretting, disbelief, a critical mind?
No temptation has surrounded you,
that the way of escape you cannot find.
God will always provide a way,
an escape so you can endure its lure.
And every temptation you suffer,
Jesus is well acquainted with we are sure.

But Deliver Us From The Evil One

And this same Savior faced,
the most evil vile foe.
Satan and his devious ploys,
at the cross he struck the mortal blow.
For the greatest evil in the history of the world,
and the saddest hour known to man.
Was the greatest triumph and victory,
that we'll spend eternity coming to understand.
So when you feel your fears,
evil, sin, or a sense of defeat.
Remember the head of the church rose again,
and has crushed the serpent's head under his feet.
In the hours and days ahead,

be bold and courageous in what is true.
Lean on the one who has defeated sin and death,
he is the Christ who will not forsake you.
No power of hell, no scheme of man,
can ever sever the love in Christ I gained that day.
For thine is the kingdom and power,
and glory forever we pray.

Ponder

Spend some time meditating on the Lord's Prayer this week (Matt 6:9–13). Think about three things: (1) It's simplicity. There is no causation or divine mysteries unraveled. Just child-like asking. (2) It's God-centeredness. God is necessary and trustworthy for everything, I am not. (3) It's clarity. No Christianese or empty phrases or grandiose requests. Just an open heart and surrender to the Father's will.

Stay

Does your prayer life feel more like a pressurized obligation, or a playful conversation? Think of the person you feel most comfortable talking to, how the conversation is easy and flows. That is God's intention when you talk to him. Just start praying by talking to him like a person who knows you, loves you, and is safe. "Good morning, Father . . . "

Pray

Psalm 143:8: "Let me hear in the morning of your steadfast love, for in you I trust. Make me know the way I should go, for to you I lift up my soul."

Romans 8:15: "For you did not receive the spirit of slavery to fall back into fear, but you have received the Spirit of adoption as sons, by whom we cry, 'Abba! Father!'"

Hebrews 5:7: "While Jesus was here on earth, he offered prayers and pleadings, with a loud cry and tears, to the one who could rescue him from death. And God heard his prayers because of his deep reverence for God." (NLT)

7. WEANED OFF WORRY

Do you carry around a burden?
A decision looming perhaps?
The inevitable unknown,
that may fall into your lap?
Are there things to do next week?
Or pains you anticipate ahead?
A fear of something tomorrow?
A scary future that you dread?
Anxiety like a rocking chair,
back and forth it goes.
It comes upon us like a wave,
knocking us backwards off our toes.
Perhaps a reassuring word,
is the calming that we need.
The groaning of the Holy Spirit,
and a Savior to intercede.
The nations rage, the kingdoms totter,
the mountains move into the sea.
But I know a God who is my refuge,
the Lord of hosts is the one with me.
I do not occupy my thoughts with things,
too great and grand for my heart.
Like a weaned child with its mother,
from my soul he'll surely not depart.
You are my hiding place and my shield,
you hold me up that I may be still.
And projecting tomorrow into today,
does not hasten me towards your will.
For who is seated at God's right hand,
far above all dominion and power?
Jesus our great high priest,
we can call upon at any hour.
All things under his feet,
head over all that he reigns.
All things created through and for him,
he is the hope that we proclaim.

So cast all your anxieties on him,
because he cares for you.
Love your neighbor, serve your friend,
in the small things be faithful and true.
For when the righteous cry for help,
his ears are towards their fears.
And as we walk in this fallen world,
our Redeemer keeps bottled our tears.
For in just a little while,
our fretting will turn into delight.
When at last we see his face,
and our faith gives way to sight.
So aspire to live quietly and mind your affairs,
And when the waters around you feel deep.
Remember the Lord is your keeper and shade,
He who keeps Israel will neither slumber nor sleep.

Ponder

Believing you are loved, cared for, and safe is the antidote to fear. Consider how the cross of Christ is meant to convince you that you are exhaustively loved, comprehensively cared for, and eternally safe.

Stay

In the power of the Spirit, remind yourself that God loves you whenever a fearful thought pops into your mind (see 1 John 4).

Pray

Psalm 27:1: "The LORD is my light and my salvation; whom shall I fear? The LORD is the stronghold of my life; of whom shall I be afraid?"

Psalm 34:4: "I sought the LORD, and he answered me and delivered me from all my fears."

1 John 4:18: "There is no fear in love, but perfect love casts out fear. For fear has to do with punishment, and whoever fears has not been perfected in love."

8. MOM GUILT

Have I done enough?
I see my faults so clear.
I want to give my kids the best,
failing and inadequacy I fear.
Some days I feel so tired,
so much to juggle, such a mess.
Did I listen? Was I helpful?
Lord, I failed another test.
I grew angry and impatient,
spent too much time on my phone.
Saw my child as a nuisance,
gave into that temptation, to wandering I am prone.
Or perhaps I was too busy,
to savor them and read.
Or I felt so overwhelmed,
to their voices and their needs.
I missed that opportunity,
when they tried calling my name.
Choosing tasks over people,
my busyness becoming my shame.
I want to be a good parent,
with children that succeed and thrive.
A house that's clean, a list that's checked,
and for our family to be happy and alive.
But so often as I finish a day,
I tend to dwell on all my faults.
My failures and sins like weights,
as I again dance this Mom-Guilt waltz.
Then the Spirit prompts me,
not to look within but without.
Where my Savior beckons me to leave,
all my burdens and my doubt.
Whispering, "Come to me all who labor,
and are heavy laden.
And I will give you rest,
my yoke is your real haven,

it is I who passed the test."
His call is for the weary,
and certainly Mom-guilt qualifies.
Refreshment and rest are found in Jesus,
for he alone can satisfy.
The law of parenting we put on ourselves,
the burden and its weight.
Cannot be lifted by more effort,
or any well-intentioned plans we create.
Perfect parenting is not the goal,
but depending, abiding, with trust.
The fruit of laying up treasures in heaven,
where there is no thief, moth, or rust.
Give Jesus your tired soul,
cry out to him with your tired eyes.
Bring Jesus all your sins and failures,
and find his mercy will be your supply.
When my heart is faint,
lead me to the rock that is higher than I.
The only ground that can hold me up,
equipping me to go and die.
As I lean on and seek his counsel,
endurance, patience, and wisdom will begin.
Transforming me in all the roles,
that he has called me to walk in.
It is finished, you've nothing to prove,
your guilt is nailed to Calvary's tree.
Now walk by faith, you're not alone,
in Jesus you're righteous and free.

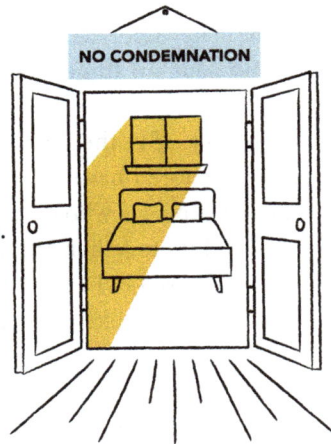

Ponder

Think about the fact that, on the cross, Jesus Christ was considered guilty for every sinful thought, word, deed, and desire you will ever commit. Even those you will never be aware of. Think about the fact that every ounce of punishment for them has already been meted out on Jesus. There are literally no debts, crimes, or transgressions on your report card. Take the week to bask in such amazing grace.

Stay

Where do you tend to feel guilty for things God doesn't hold you responsible for? Where do you tend to feel guilty for too long for things you are responsible for? If you're wrestling with the difference between good conviction and false guilt, ask a trusted friend to help you discern. Ask them to pray with you.

Pray

Isaiah 6:6: "Then one of the seraphim flew to me, having in his hand a burning coal that he had taken with tongs from the altar. And he touched my mouth and said: 'Behold, this has touched your lip; your guilt is taken away, and your sin atoned for.'"

Isaiah 50:7–9: "But the Lord God helps me; therefore I have not been disgraced; therefore I have set my face like a flint, and I know that I shall not be put to shame. He who vindicates me is near. Who will contend with me? Let us stand up together. Who is my adversary? Let him come near to me. Behold, the Lord GOD helps me; who will declare me guilty? Behold, all of them will wear out like a garment; the moth will eat them up."

1 Corinthians 1:7–9: " . . . as you wait for the revealing of our Lord Jesus Christ, who will sustain you to the end, guiltless in the day of our Lord Jesus Christ. God is faithful, by whom you were called into the fellowship of his Son, Jesus Christ our Lord."

9. A PRAYER REGARDING POWER

Whatever is true, whatever is just,
whatever is lovely and pure.
Commendable and worthy of excellence,
Lord, these are leaders we implore.
No candidate will be perfect,
no policy will make us whole.
So, we vote in faith and hold loosely,
knowing Jesus opened the scroll.
The King's heart is a stream of water,
in the Lord's right hand.
He turns it wherever he will,
every ruler before him will stand.
Put not your trust in princes,
in a son of man, whom salvation won't come.
When his breath departs, he returns to earth,
and on that very day his plans are undone.
Render to Caesar the things that are Caesar's,
to God-given authority we must yield.
But render to God the things that are God's,
for before the King of Kings all will kneel.
Our hope is not in parents or presidents,
yet our responsibilities we must keep.
The powerful called to promote good and punish evil,
we pray they know which is which as they lead.
Reasonable, clear-minded, just, and steady,
not ambitious for selfish power.
Lord, be pleased to raise up those who're ready,
we depend on you this sacred hour.

Ponder

Who are the people you feel have abused their power and authority? Whether toward you personally or more generally? Be reminded that all their power and authority came from God. Therefore, either Jesus paid for their evil or they will be held accountable on judgment day. Consider how this frees you from the poison of anger, bitterness, and revenge.

Stay

Are you more prone to look at authority figures (presidents, parents, teachers, coaches, bosses) as divine or demonic? Do you tend to view them as saviors or with cynicism? There may be good reasons for your tendency, but ask the Lord to help give you the balance Jesus had—to honor authorities without worshiping or dismissing them.

Pray

Psalm 146:3-7, "Put not your trust in princes, in a son of man, in whom there is no salvation. When his breath departs, he returns to the earth; on that very day his plans perish. Blessed is he whose help is the God of Jacob, whose hope is in the LORD his God, who made heaven and earth, the sea, and all that is in them, who keeps faith forever; who executes justice for the oppressed, who gives food to the hungry..."

Acts 5:29, "But Peter and the apostles answered, 'We must obey God rather than men.'"

1 Peter 2:13-17, "Be subject for the Lord's sake to every human institution, whether it be to the emperor as supreme, or to governors as sent by him to punish those who do evil and to praise those who do good. For this is the will of God, that by doing good you should put to silence the ignorance of foolish people. Live as people who are free, not using your freedom as a cover-up for evil, but living as servants of God. Honor everyone. Love the brotherhood. Fear God. Honor the emperor."

10. SITTING IN STILLNESS

Sometimes I have a moment,
to sit and think and dwell.
Before the chaos enters in,
and my children's needs begin to swell.
How do I steward these times,
that I don't often get to spend?
Clean a room, scrub a floor,
conquer my list, run an errand?
So tempting to tackle and squeeze in,
a task I need to complete.
Because soon they will come and find me,
I need to get moving on my feet.
Who can focus with people around,
especially children whose needs are many?
For once you string up one bead,
the others fall off in plenty.
There will always be something to do,
to keep chaos from my life and home.
But perhaps today I can accomplish more,
if I choose the better portion in my moment alone.

Instead of trying to get ahead,
by much activity and tasks.
I may in the end accomplish more,
as I settle my heart and ask.
If I make no room for God,
drowning him out with hustle and bustle.
I lose the gain of a settled soul,
and shrink my meditating muscle.
Rather than scrolling my phone,
perhaps I can hold a book in hand.
Turn its pages, smell its ink,
look out my window and understand.
Pray for someone that I love,
or stay on one topic and deeply think.
Be still and keep a quiet heart,

and let thoughts of God just sink.
We're so afraid of silence,
and being with our thoughts alone.
But often this is where God meets us,
in our stillness he can be known.
To be clear God is always with us,
in the mundane and the stress.
He loves us as we conquer tasks,
he loves us nonetheless.
Serving has its place,
we need to work, toil, and labor.
But being distracted with much serving,
can hinder the better portion we must savor.
No doubt there is much to be anxious over,
and it feels more constructive to be on our feet.
But I wonder if sitting, savoring, and thinking,
can be the better portion we need to eat.
Be still before the Lord and wait patiently,
let his word and Spirit fill the space.
Let go of control by exertion,
remember to quietly seek his grace.
Running the race with endurance,
requires moments of stagnation.
In our slowing down we're speeding up,
as we make Christ our quiet foundation.
So the next afternoon that is open,
or the next ten minutes allotted to you.
Sit, think, ponder, and give space,
to think on your Savior and what is true.
The Lord will refresh and restore you,
in a much deeper and lasting way.
When you become comfortable with stillness,
you put the God who is in control on display.

Ponder

Read Revelation chapter 4. We find God's heavenly throne described as, "before the throne there was as it were a sea of glass, like crystal" (Rev 4:6). The image evokes a sense of stillness, calm, and peace. While your life may feel like a hurricane, from God's perspective everything is going perfectly according to plan. How can that reality give you comfort in the chaos?

Stay

Is being still, quiet, or alone hard for you? How can the reality that Jesus did the work and fulfilled the law free you to enjoy God more and worry less? How does his death and resurrection motivate you to fulfill your responsibilities but also assure you that it's not all up to you?

Pray

Psalm 131:2: "But I have calmed and quieted my soul, like a weaned child with its mother; like a weaned child is my soul within me."

Isaiah 30:15: "For thus said the Lord GOD, the Holy One of Israel, In returning and rest you shall be saved; in quietness and in trust shall be your strength."

Luke 10:41: "But the Lord answered her, 'Martha Martha, you are anxious and troubled about many things, but one thing is necessary. Mary has chosen the good portion, which will not be taken away from her.'"

11. CONCERNING MARRIAGE

The glazed over look,
the wedding day,
It's here!! It's here, you sigh.
You get to marry the one you love,
as you blissfully look into his eyes.
Your stomachs turning all in knots,
You smile so much it hurts your face.
But you don't care it's your wedding day,
Keep this moment, slow down the pace.
You are ready to love this person,
finally get to be with them everyday.
No more goodbyes, no distance between,
it will be so wonderful this way.
You're glad you know you're a sinner,
and that your spouse surely is too.
You will have words, at times disagree,
and get in an argument or two.
Yet God will help you, he always will,
his business is to grow you in grace.
As you study his word, as you pray and repent,
the growth in your marriage will race.
Remember to always say good night,
don't let the sun go down while your heart is cold.
Cultivate friendship, do things they like to do,
even things you can still do as you grow old.
Take the time to listen and ask questions,
rather than hearing yourself speak.
Plan special times to pray together,
at least one day a week.
Invite friends, invite strangers,
open up your home to many.
Care for each other, study each other,
know weaknesses and strengths—there'll be plenty!
If children come along,
they will steal your heart and time it's true.
But remember whose heart God calls you to first,

after Jesus, your spouse is the one to pursue.
Don't take it lightly, do not give up,
the grass on that side is not as green as it seems.
Marriage models Christ and his Bride,
therefore it glorifies God most extreme.
The world will tell you lies, the world will try to suck you in,
Fight hard with truth, the truth of his word, when temptations start to spin.
Remember your first love is Christ,
remember what he's done for you.
Extend that same mercy and love to one another,
especially when it's hard to do.
Keep your eyes on the cross,
and remember the first one to say sorry wins.
God opposes the proud but gives grace to the humble,
if it's genuine within.
Be each other's biggest fan,
encourage with your words every day.
Pray for them, romance them,
and sometimes just be a friend and play.
You get to have this privilege,
of walking in marriage hand-in-hand.
As you both walk towards the horizon,
becoming like Jesus—that's his plan.

Ponder

Think on the beautiful qualities of marriage. Think on the beautiful qualities of the gospel. How do they overlap?

Stay

To the almost married: Identify one area of selfishness that needs to die so your fiancé can live.

To the already married: What did you love to do with your spouse when you first got married? What bonded you together emotionally, spiritually, and physically? How can you wisely move toward experiencing God's grace in these areas again?

Pray

Ecclesiastes 9:7–9: "Go, eat your bread with joy, and drink your wine with a merry heart, for God has already approved what you do. Let your garments be always white. Let not oil be lacking on your head. Enjoy life with the wife whom you love, all the days of your vain life that he has given you under the sun . . . "

Song of Solomon 5:16: "His mouth is sweetness itself; he is desirable in every way. Such, O women of Jerusalem, is my lover, my friend."(NLT)

Ephesians 5:21: "Submit to one another out of reverence for Christ." (NIV)

12. DUTY AND DELIGHT

Duty versus delight,
where does one distinguish each?
"I get to" instead of "I have to,"
is always within my reach.
I get to wake up another morning,
I get to work my job.
I get to clean my home,
rather than complaining they're slobs.
Delight in my dishes,
delight during my drive.
Duty weighs me down,
whereas delight helps me thrive.
Delight in seeing this person,
delight to call my friend.
Duty yells its boisterous call,
but I refuse to condescend.
Delight in my circumstances,
even in thorns I can find a rose.
Duty wants to rob my joy,
and thoughts of drudgery to impose.
Delight to change a diaper,
delight when (again) I need to cook.
Delight in God's creation,
sipping coffee and reading a book.
Delight to see the good in others,
even when they are thorns in my side.
Delight to gaze upon Jesus Christ,
as the cross empties me of pride.
Duty that is moral and empty,
spilling over to dread and groans.
Is one of Satan's oldest tactics,
to make us feel alone.
Tempting us to think,
God is holding out on us.
How dare he give me this task,
as we fight, resist, and cuss.

But enter in from Jesse,
a branch that bears much fruit.
The Spirit of the Lord upon him,
wisdom, understanding from this shoot.
Jesus passed every test we fail,
in God's commandments he took delight.
And in any duty he was called to,
our Savior's heart was always right.
When tempted to give in,
and grasp the world and all its power.
Instead he trusted the Father's will,
pleasing him in every hour.
Familiar with all temptations we face,
a chance to begrudgingly obey.
But the joy of the Lord was his strength,
as he looked to his reward one day.
And only through the power,
of this risen, ruling, King.
Can duty become delight,
as to his cross we cling.
Lowliness, servant-hood,
being last not first.
The dryness of looking inward,
will never quench our thirst.
And even when it's hard,
our heart, just a bruised reed.
He will never break you,
and will always faithfully intercede.
For only through the gospel truth,
that we are his delight.
Will we be fueled and driven,
to continue in this fight.
Delight because I'm not guilty,
delight that I'm a new creation.
Delight because my ledger is clear,
delight for he is my salvation.
Delight that because I'm adopted,
Jesus is my brother and my friend.

Delight that this life is a vapor,
and one day this fallen world will end.
Delight because there are promises,
his word holds out for me to take.
Delight that all will be made right,
and on that promise everything I can stake.
Delight that I am loved and forgiven,
a child of God, sanctified, redeemed.
Do I have any reasons to delight?
Yes, Jesus has made me free indeed.

Ponder

As the Puritans put it, our chief end is to "glorify God and enjoy him forever." Think about how it glorifies God when you enjoy him in all things. How does finding delight in his creation and his promises bring glory to his name?

Stay

What callings in your life feel like drudgery right now? What is a potential source of delight in that calling that can bring God glory and bring you contentment?

Pray

2 Samuel 22:20: "He brought me out into a broad place; he rescued me, because he delighted in me."

Psalm 37:3–4: "Trust in the LORD, and do good; dwell in the land and befriend faithfulness. Delight yourself in the LORD, and he will give you the desires of your heart."

Matthew 13:44: "The kingdom of heaven is like treasure hidden in a field, which a man found and covered up. Then in his joy he goes and sells all that he has and buys that field."

13. MERCIFUL TO ENEMIES

Do good to those who hate you,
to those who curse you; bless.
Pray for those who mistreat you,
when they strike your cheek; rest.
Offer them your other cheek,
and if they take your stuff.
Give them even more,
though you feel it is enough.
And if someone should beg from you,
or steal your possessions away.
Do not demand them back,
put compassion on display.
If you love those who love you,
is the benefit to you so great?
Lovable people are easy to love,
the challenge is to love those we hate.
Lend and be generous,
not because you secretly hope.
For a "thank you" or something in return,
resist this slippery slope.
Love your enemies and do good,
lend, give, bless, and pray.
And when you expect no return,
your reward will be great one day.
Sons and daughters of the Most High,
to the ungrateful and evil he is kind.
Be merciful as your Father is merciful,
this is a calling that we've been assigned.
Thank you Jesus for the gift,
of living a life of mercy for me.
I hide in you when my flesh fails,
Lord give me a heart for my enemy.

Ponder

Take some time to consider the amazing mercies of God. He forgives everything you've ever done wrong, and everything you should have done right. Not only that, but Jesus shares the inheritance he's earned with you. He makes enemies into family, forever.

Stay

Is there someone in your life you feel is against you? Perhaps without a good reason? How can you surprise them with mercy? What specific word or deed might draw them toward Jesus, as they see you go the extra mile for them?

Pray

Joel 2:13: "Return to the LORD your God, for he is gracious and merciful, slow to anger, and abounding in steadfast love; and he relents over disaster."

Galatians 6:9: "And let us not grow weary of doing good, for in due season we will reap, if we do not give up."

Luke 6:27–36: "But I say to you who hear, Love your enemies, do good to those who hate you, bless those who curse you, pray for those who abuse you. To the one who strikes you on the cheek, offer the other also, and from one who takes away your cloak do not withhold your tunic either. Give to everyone who begs from you, and from one who takes away your goods do not demand them back."

14. CREATURE COMFORTS

I want a dose of comfort,
just a little silence please.
A day filled with my pleasures,
a cup of coffee with a dash of ease.
I want my house this way,
I want a holiday to this place.
Just a day where I feel good,
from my people some extra space.
A rest day would be nice,
even a nap would serve me fine.
Oh how inconvenient to my rest,
are these children and grandchildren of mine.
It's like they plan a needy rebellion,
the moment I talk on the phone.
The bathroom is suddenly the play room,
when all I want is to shower alone.
They know just when to spill the drink,
ransack a room and provoke visual stress.
Start bickering when I settle into a project,
or escalate talking and banging in excess.
A sassy attitude to a simple direction,
a conflict to referee when I feel weak.
An unexpected sickness,
interrupts the comfort that I seek.
A breakdown in a moment,
I need to focus and hit send.
Their timeliness impeccable,
some days, Lord when will it end?
But then the Holy Spirit,
nudges my self-focused heart.
And whispers and convicts me,
my paradigm is dark.
For opportunities surround me,
a cry, a spill, a snarky remark.
Stop me from self-absorption,
and give me a purpose to embark.

My ministry to my children or grandchildren,
is not only when all is well.
But is most effective in the chaos,
as I calm and tend the waves that swell.
Caring for their little hearts,
no doubt takes away from "me."
But as I pour more into them,
from my selfishness I'm set free.
Serving should not only come,
when it's in my time or in my way.
For the nature of true serving,
is to give one's life away.
Serving requires sacrifice,
as I die a bit more to my pride.
For in losing my life I gain it,
as I walk by Jesus' side.
Myself, me-time, isolation,
become our idol if we start to demand.
Because even if we get our comfort,
we won't enjoy the result if selfishly planned.
Constant comfort reaching,
will always keep it out of our grasp.
While the lessons of serving our neighbor,
will always give us something that lasts.
And the motivation to keep going,
is Gospel love that purchased me.
For the blood of Jesus is powerful enough,
to destroy my comfort idols and make me free.
True comfort, rest, and refreshment,
are found in Christ and him alone.
The God of all comfort in our affliction,
has declared through Jesus we are his own.
One day you will receive your reward,
the fruit of your labors a harvest to his name.
God sees when the work is uncomfortable,
your serving is not overlooked or done in vain.
So next time a little one bumps your comfort,
by discouraging your ambitions for your day.

Trust his hand is changing your heart,
especially when children get in the way.
As you lay down your own comfort,
God will give you every grace and blessing you need.
And you may be surprised that deeper peace,
transcends external comforts that you seek.

Ponder

Think about several people who have sacrificed significantly to do good to you. What has that meant to you? What if they had taken the easier path of their own comfort? Take time to praise God for them this week.

Stay

What are some of your favorite creature comforts? Knowing these are often good things God has gladly given us, have any become too big in your heart? Where your mind drifts toward them constantly. Where you don't just want them but must have them. Where if they are threatened or taken away, you react with fear, anxiety, or anger. Take time to talk to God about any idols he reveals.

Pray

Psalm 119:50: "This is my comfort in my affliction, that your promise gives me life."

Ezekiel 36:25–28: "I will sprinkle clean water on you, and you shall be clean from all your uncleanness, and from all your idols I will cleanse you. And I will give you a new heart, and a new spirit I will put within you. And I will remove the heart of stone from your flesh and give you a heart of flesh. And I will put my Spirit within you, and cause you to walk in my statutes and be careful to obey my rules . . . you shall be my people, and I will be your God."

1 John 5:21: "Little children, keep yourselves from idols."

15. THE FRUIT OF THE SPIRIT

Love—The ultimate fruit of faith,
the character of the Godhead three in one.

Joy—Transcends our circumstances,
a deep contentment in the Son.

Peace—We're no longer enemies,
reconciled to God and others by the blood he shed.

Patience—We follow God's timetable,
enduring now and what lies ahead.

Kindness—We extend sympathy, compassion, and
generosity without exception.

Goodness—We seek to bless others,
purely, without deception.

Faithfulness—Do what you say you will,
let your "yes" be yes and your "no" be no.

Gentleness—A soft word, a tender touch,
Christ's lowliness of heart we show.

Self-Control—We resist our sin,
we don't give in, we pass the test.

This fruit comes from the Spirit's gardening,
creating in us and through us a harvest of spiritual rest.

So before you speak, before you read,
before you scroll or write.

Before you speak behind closed doors,
ask God to make your heart pure and contrite.

Against these things there is NO LAW,
to his saints the Lord delights to give.

So let us resist the deadly desires of the flesh,
and by the Holy Spirit be led and live.

Ponder

Meditate on the amazing truth that if you belong to Christ, you "have cruci-fied the flesh with its passions and desires." You are now more fundamen-tally a saint than a sinner. You have heart of flesh, not a heart of stone.

Stay

Which fruit of the Spirit in your life can you praise God for this week? How are you (even by small degrees) not the person you used to be? Thank God for tending the garden of your heart.

Pray

Ezekiel 11:19–20: "And I will give them one heart, and a new spirit I will put within them. I will remove the heart of stone from their flesh and give them a heart of flesh, that they may walk in my statutes and keep my rules and obey them. And they shall be my people, and I will be their God."

Luke 6:43–45: "For no good tree bears bad fruit, nor again does a bad tree bear good fruit, for each tree is known by its own fruit. For figs are not gath-ered from thornbushes, nor are grapes picked from a bramble bush. The good person out of the good treasure of his heart produces good, and the evil person out of his evil treasure produces evil, for out of the abundance of the heart his mouth speaks."

Galatians 5:16–18: "But I say, walk by the Spirit, and you will not gratify the desires of the flesh. For the desires of the flesh are against the Spirit, and the desires of the Spirit are against the flesh, for these are opposed to each other, to keep you from doing the things you want to do. But if you are led by the Spirit, you are not under the law."

16. SERVE AND PRAY, LOVE AND STAY

I see your faults and weaknesses,
the mess you leave around.
Your quirks and insufficiency,
there is ample muck that can be found.
I see you're clumsy and lazy,
selfish and filled with pride.
Your blind spots in so many areas,
in our home it's hard to hide.
I see how you struggle,
I see your sins besetting.
Yet, I love you anyway,
in this I have no regretting.
Love is not merely an emotion,
but a decision that I will stay.
My commitment to you overriding,
any confusion that is in play.
Any heated arguments, disagreements,
or blame that is transferred.
Even when you don't like me,
I refuse to let pride get the last word.
Staying, loving, immovable,
grabbing my anchor when it gets tough.
And my past commitment vows,
are what need to be enough.
The vows are what keep us,
not the other way around.
I will never let you push me away,
no matter how bleak our present found.
I'll love and stay, I'll die and pray,
I'll choose the better route.
I won't give up, I will not quit,
my love for you is never in doubt.
For I see you and I love you,
and I see the horizon where you'll be.
Conformed, sanctified, made new,
reaching the peak of your glory.

I want to carry you through the journey,
and stay with you until the end.
I will hold your hand and heart,
this is one promise I'll extend.
The gospel explains marriage,
marriage explains gospel love and grace.
When God invented marriage,
he already had his saving work in place.
While we were enemies of God,
still sinners, ungodly, and weak.
At the right time Jesus died for us,
his reconciliation now what we speak.
This kind of love fuels our marriages,
loving despite what we feel.
We who were hating and running from God,
have been loved with a love fierce and real.
Replace all the above with "God,"
and see exactly how God relates to you.
He loves, He stays, He died, He prays,
for those in Jesus this is all true.

Ponder

We are told it's OK (even healthy) to walk away from a marriage if we don't feel "in love" anymore. Are inner feelings a reliable guide to happiness? Why do we make vows without escape clauses on our wedding day?

Stay

Ask your spouse how you can pray for them this week. Report back how God led those prayers at the end of the week.

Pray

Psalm 119:130, 133: "The unfolding of your words gives light . . . Keep steady my steps according to your promise, and let no iniquity get dominion over me."

John 17:17: "Sanctify them in the truth; your word is truth."

1 Thessalonians 5:13–15: "Be at peace among yourselves. And we urge you, brothers, admonish the idle, encourage the fainthearted, help the weak, be patient with them all. See that no one repays anyone evil for evil, but always seek to do good to one another and to everyone."

17. PERFORMANCE

A whirlwind of emotions,
has settled in my mind.
A perfect day of performance,
is difficult for me to find.
Today I did not live in the Proverbs,
where all seems to go just right.
I lived in Ecclesiastes,
where futility was my plight.
The project I wanted to start,
blew up in my face.
My attitude began slipping,
my heart quickly a disgrace.
My children felt my frustration,
as I barked at them as well.
The good intentions for my day,
were drowned, collapsed, and fell.
Normally a successful day,
is when I measure up to my bar.
Nailed that chore and got it done,
parented my kids like a rock star.
When I'm responding well to things,
proud and patting myself on the back.
For all my good deeds and attitudes,
man I'm right on track.
But whether my day was complete,
or I seemed to fall flat on my face.
Pride is a sneaky and clever one,
and can slip in without a trace.
On a good day he loves to proclaim,
what a good lad or lass I am.
Look at you go!
but his facade hides from me a sham.
For why is it that you boast,
if everything you have is received?
Boast in the Lord who became wisdom,
righteousness to you who believed.

A proficient day is not a bad thing,
received with a grateful heart of praise.
But you did not earn more favor,
from the one who was raised.
Jesus loves you on good days,
because he's prepared them for you.
And all your noble endeavors,
did not add an ounce to what is true.
But another way that tricky pride,
can make you feel displaced,
Is taking your days of discouragement,
and making you feel a sense of disgrace.
I failed again, I messed it up,
I sinned, guilty as charged.
Comeour persistent thoughts,
looming painstakingly large.
It's in these moments you must recall,
that Jesus loves you still the same.
There is no work you've failed to do,
that will make him turn from you in shame.
You see his blood has cleansed you,
reckoned you as wicked no more.
Our iniquities and transgressions forgiven,
to the Father you are restored.
Once you are found in him,
the Spirit is your inheritance guaranteed.
So however today went my friend,
in Jesus you are safe and free.
Remember this when you fail again,
repent and turn if this you must do.
Yet know his mercies are new each morn,
and he delights when you run to him too.
You are in Jesus becoming,
the person you already are declared to be.
As you run the race with endurance,
he will sanctify and make you holy.
So shake off the chains of performance,
Christ performed in your place instead.

The gospel assures you of grace,
and turns your efforts on their head.
When Christ appears on that day,
you shall be like him indeed.
Because you will see him as he is,
no failure can this truth impede.

Ponder

Consider how the good news of the gospel is the only message powerful enough to free you from the twin temptations of pride ("I did well, people praised me, I feel good about myself") and despair ("I failed, people criticized me, I feel bad about myself").

Stay

Where in life are you hard on yourself? Where do you feel you can never quite measure up? Confess your unbelief in the gospel and receive the good news again that Jesus measured up for you. Receive the truth that in God's eyes, in Christ, it is just as if you've never sinned and just as if you've always obeyed.

Pray

John 19:30: "When Jesus had received the sour wine, he said, 'It is finished,' and he bowed his head and gave up his spirit."

Romans 8:2–3: "For the law of the Spirit of life has set you free in Christ Jesus from the law of sin and death. For God has done what the law, weakened by the flesh, could not do."

Galatians 5:1: "For freedom Christ has set us free; stand firm therefore, and do not submit again to a yoke of slavery."

Please and Thank You when you ask,
enough trust to ask just one time.
Let the family enjoy their meal,
before you ask for seconds is truly kind.
Ask good questions, listen well,
take an interest in someone and their day.
Be slow to speak and quick to hear,
and invested in the conversation stay.
If the food is not your favorite,
refrain from saying so.
Choose contentment over and over,
for there seeds of gratitude you will sow.
Laugh lots, sing together,
the family table is the place.
Where joys and sorrows freely flow,
the air of conversation is the Spirit and his grace.
As the years go by meal after meal,
the high chairs are no more.
Mom and Dad start to wrinkle,
and little legs touch the floor.
We hope our Savior will be more treasured,
around this table every year.
The love of God and all his goodness,
bringing more and more gospel cheer.
Food, story-telling, or just sitting quietly in thought,
each is a cure for weariness, sadness, and fear.
Blessings that our Lord has wrought.

Ponder

Imagine a table full of people sharing a meal in your home. What are some
of the beautiful things happening in that moment? Think of the Passover
meal for Israel, Jesus eating with tax collectors and sinners, the Lord's Sup-
per in the church, and the marriage supper of the Lamb when he returns.

Stay

What are specific things you would like to change during meal times to make them more rich and encouraging? It might be meal prep and food choices. It might be everyone at the table together. It might be prayer and singing. It might be an extra chair for friends and guests. It might be thoughtful, interesting, and playful conversation. Recognizing it will take time and intentionality to cultivate table culture.

Pray

Deuteronomy 16:1–2: "In honor of the LORD your God, celebrate the Passover each year in the early spring, in the month of Abib, for that was the month in which the LORD your God brought you out of Egypt by night. Your Passover sacrifice may be from either the flock or the herd, and it must be sacrificed to the LORD your God at the designated place of worship—the place he chooses for his name to be honored." (NLT)

Luke 15:1–2: "Now the tax collectors and sinners were all drawing near to hear him. And the Pharisees and the scribes grumbled, saying, "This man receives sinners and eats with them.""

Acts 2:46–47: "And day by day, attending the temple together and breaking bread in their homes, they received their food with glad and generous hearts, praising God and having favor with all the people. And the Lord added to their number day by day those who were being saved."

19. GODWARD NOT SELFWARD

Everything in our culture,
drives us further into "me."
The head-to-toe mirrors at the gym,
my camera flipping to selfie.
Take self-care time, you need it,
if it feels good do it, don't wait.
But has anyone sat back,
to consider what this creates?
Self-absorption, self-obsession,
is nothing new under the sun.
We have just made it acceptable,
something good, something fun.
And while it's true we have dignity,
worth, in the image of God we're made.
A self-obsessed heart and mind,
is not a sustainable charade.
The world is not about "me,"
what I want and my great name.
The Creator, Redeemer, Judge, and King,
deserves all the glory that I claim.
Do nothing from selfish ambition,
in humility count others more great.
If anyone thinks he is something,
when he is nothing, deceit is his bait.
Thinking of ourselves more highly,
does not position us for grace.
But we have a helper beside us,
who runs toward us when we're displaced.
The one who is high and lifted up,
inhabits eternity, holy without doubt.
Our God who deserves all accolades,
and it is him this world is about.
And rather than staying lofty,
far, unreachable, and cold.
He condescended and moved towards us,
in the greatest story ever told.

A story of redemption,
written on every page of his book.
A rescue plan of healing,
for all the wrong turns our heart took.
We don't need more of us,
looking inside makes us empty.
Jesus came and was lifted up,
to grant us forgiveness and joys plenty.
Incline our heart to your testimonies,
and not to selfish gain.
Let Jesus' perfect life and death,
propel us outside ourselves and to His reign.
And less of us and more of Christ,
creates joy beyond all measure.
May he increase and I decrease,
Lord, may you continually be my treasure.

Ponder

How is a life spent focused on God and others better than a life focused on yourself? Think about how Jesus lived the most fulfilled life possible for a human being and was always self-forgetful and outward focused.

Stay

When is self-care and introspection a good thing? When might it go too far?

Pray

Isaiah 57:15: "For thus says the One who is high and lifted up, who inhabits eternity, whose name is Holy: I dwell in the high and holy place, and also with him who is of a contrite and lowly spirit, to revive the spirit of the lowly, and to revive the heart of the contrite."

John 3:30: "He must increase, but I must decrease."

Galatians 6:3: "For if anyone thinks he is something, when he is nothing, he deceives himself."

20. OUT OF THE MOUTH

Do you have a child,
or perhaps this could be you?
Stream of consciousness overflows,
and too many words ensue?
When words are many from our mouths,
transgression is not far away.
But whoever restrains his lips is prudent,
even if they have much to say.
Words always have meaning,
punch that flows from our hearts.
So as you parent and shape their words,
this may be a thoughtful start.
And remember as you shepherd them,
God desires to shepherd you too.
The apple may not fall far from the tree,
the Spirit will also help restore you.
Let no corrupting talk,
come out of your mouth today.
But only such as for building up,
that fits the occasion come what may.
Do these words bless my sister?
Do these words edify my brother?
Are they timely and fitting,
in conversation I have with another?
Do these words give grace,
to the ones that read or hear?
Do they leave the person I'm with,
filled up with hope and cheer?
A word in season how good it is,
and persuasiveness comes with sweetness of speech.
The heart of the wise makes his speech judicious,
and discerning lips are within his reach.
And when our child's words or ours,
pour out like a fire hose.
We mimic a fool who takes no pleasure to understand,
but only to impose.

Recall how the heart of the righteous ponders,
how to answer before he speaks.
And sadly the art of listening,
is less common and more unique.
To give an answer before we hear,
is to our folly and shame.
As we help our child, God helps us,
to give them the promises he proclaims.
For though, "Woe is me! For I am lost;
for I am a man of unclean lips," is conceded.
Yet the burning coal has touched my mouth,
and applied the atoning grace I needed.
The purest lips in all the world,
when accused did not open to defend.
As a sheep before its shearers is silent,
Jesus' perfect response I can't comprehend.
From his lips came the words, "Go in peace,
daughter, your faith has made you well.
And from his lips he calmed their hearts,
even as he calmed the waters as they swelled.
He uttered, "Father forgive them,
they know not what they do."
And to the thief on the cross that believed,
"Today in paradise I will be with you."
Creation only needed,
one word from Him and it came to pass.
Surely he can tame my tongue,
when my words are flying out fast.
And the epicenter of our words,
resides in the chambers of our heart.
If we ask the Spirit for help,
he will come with grace to impart.
Our words can begin to bring life,
healing, wisdom, and soothing so sweet.
A timely and comforting balm,
if God's own words we take and eat.

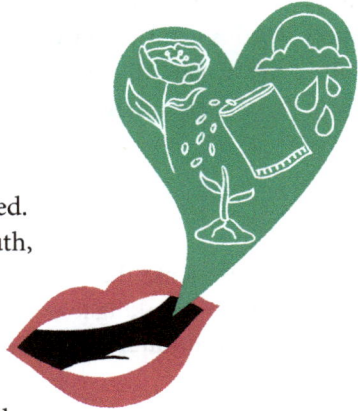

Ponder

Consider the truth that the God of the Bible is a God who speaks and listens. Every word in Scripture is chosen and spoken with infinite wisdom, *for you*. Every word is a gift of perfect love, *for you*. He listens to your every word with perfect patience, compassionate understanding, and gracious care, *every day*. Reflect on the privilege of knowing such a wonderful person.

Stay

Where do you sense the Lord wanting to conform your speech to the likeness of Christ? Speaking less? Listening more? Asking good questions? Being willing to communicate more often and more deeply, in love?

Pray

Matthew 12:35–37: "The good person out of his good treasure brings forth good, and the evil person out of his evil treasure brings forth evil. I tell you, on the day of judgment people will give account for every careless word they speak, for by your words you will be justified, and by your words you will be condemned."

Luke 4:20–22: " . . . And the eyes of all in the synagogue were fixed on him. And he began to say to them, 'Today this Scripture has been fulfilled in your hearing.' And all spoke well of him and marveled at the gracious words that were coming from his mouth."

2 Timothy 3:16: "All Scripture is breathed out by God and profitable for teaching, for reproof, for correction, and for training in righteousness, that the man of God may be complete, equipped for every good work."

21. A LONG OBEDIENCE

The day has dawned and as I sit,
and fall into a heap.
I think about how tired,
are my body and my feet.
I did not change the world today,
no lofty goals were met.
No one noticed what I did,
so much I haven't finished yet.
The compliments I yearned for,
never once did hit my ears.
I am pretty sure no one said thank you,
I had a moment on the verge of tears.
My ambitions to do something else,
creep slowly to my mind.
God, I don't want what you've given,
that thing over there seems a better find.
When these thoughts start to creep,
and discontent rears its ugly head.
There are a few places I can go,
and thoughts I need instead.
Instead of craving honor, glory,
and praise that resounds back to me.
I can choose to embrace joy,
meekness, lowliness and obscurity.
To be high is to be low,
to be first is to be last.
To be served is to serve,
to be honored is to be steadfast.
Whom have I in heaven but you?
and there is nothing upon earth I see.
That surpasses all the treasure and worth,
of how my Savior Jesus has set me free.
Free to keep my grandeur plans,
ambitions, goals and dreams.
Underneath his providential care,
and within the plan he deems.

Sufficient for today and tomorrow,
is what is in front of me now.
To walk in faithful steadfastness,
and to let Christ show me how.
For he has done it perfectly,
finished the race, obeyed in my stead.
Given his Spirit to empower me,
to faithfully walk on ahead.
The mundane things have significance,
the deeds of sacrifice, kindness and love.
Patience, endurance, steadfastness,
kindness, self-control all from above.
Faithfulness is not so cool,
the world sees it as weak and bland.
It may not give you accolades,
or an audience that is grand.
But if you're in Christ, God sees you,
he knows your heart strings oh so deep.
He promises to be faithful to you,
despite the goodness you can't keep.
Long obedience in the right direction,
in those things that no one else sees.
Be faithful with what he gives to you,
lean on Jesus in whom He's well pleased.
Faithfulness over time,
one day, one moment at a time enjoy.
Staying in the present,
not letting anxious thoughts destroy.
For tomorrow is none of our business,
God's already there so we don't have to be.
Faithfulness today and over time,
is the key to rest and being free.

Ponder

Think of some specific ways God has been faithful to you over the years. Physically, spiritually, emotionally, relationally, and financially. Will he ever change? Will he abandon you?

Stay

Where is God calling you to stretch beyond your comfort zone? Where can you stick with someone over the long haul as God has stuck with you?

Pray

Deuteronomy 32:4: "The Rock, his work is perfect, for all his ways are justice. A God of faithfulness and without iniquity, just and upright is he."

1 Corinthians 1:9: "God is faithful, by whom you were called into the fellowship of his Son, Jesus Christ our Lord."

2 Timothy 2:11–13: "The saying is trustworthy, for: If we have died with him, we will also live with him; if we endure, we will also reign with him; if we deny him, he also will deny us; if we are faithless, he remains faithful— for he cannot deny himself."

22. MOMS NEED JESUS TOO

"Please forgive me darlings,"
as I snuggled them to bed.
"Mommy yelled a lot today,"
I confessed as chaos filled my head.
Their neediness was amplified,
it seemed it never ceased.
Interruptions all day long,
whining, crying, asking just increased.
And though these things provoked me,
the problem was my own.
For their neediness gave occasion,
for my heart idols to be shown.
But as I lay down next to them,
confessing all my sin.
My daughter looked into my eyes,
and hugged me as she grinned.
"Mommy, I love you so much,
you're the best Mommy in the world to me."
It was as though the Lord just knew,
of the reassurance which I had need.
Had you been a fly on the wall,
and observed me on that day.
Mother of the year award?
more like "worst mom" is what you'd say.
I didn't embrace interruptions,
I didn't count it a joy.
To help them with their problems,
or be patient with their ploys.
I wanted to run away,
be alone, have time to recharge.
And when my demands were not met,
the sin produced from me was large.
Yet before the evening approached,
the Lord's word came to my mind:
"How did that desire go today,
when comfort you did not find?"

Convicted of my craving,
for the comfort and rest I didn't get.
A good thing got too big,
so my heart began to anger and fret.
Mama, when this moment comes,
and the Spirit slaps you in the face.
His reminder is the smelling salt,
that wakes you up to his grace.
Grace abundant that he gives,
available and ready for you.
At any moment of the day,
to lead you to what's beautiful and true.
Ask him for forgiveness,
confess craving comfort for yourself.
Being served over serving others,
leaving sacrifice up on the shelf.
An anguished cry, a drawn out moan,
whether it's a whisper or a yelp.
Create in me a clean heart oh Lord!
or just a simple, "Help!"
I thank the Lord that on that day,
he gave me what I needed.
Even though I was a wretch,
up until the hour that I pleaded.
To turn my course was oh so sweet,
new joy infused into my hardened heart.
The callings God had given that day,
began to take on a fresh new start.
And as I heard my daughter,
say those words to me that night.
Underneath her sweet smile,
was my Savior's great delight.
The Lord is near the brokenhearted,
and saves the crushed in spirit I know.
And I felt him remind me once again:
"My daughter, I love you so.
Though your sin, dear child,
has pierced my side today.

The love that held me to the cross,
has taken all your guilt away.
Just as your child is dependent,
on your help, love, and embrace.
So you are dependent on my power,
my faithfulness, and my infinite grace."
So struggling mom, discouraged mom,
weak mom who knows her need.
You are the mom that Jesus hears,
and for you he'll intercede.
When you see their neediness,
think on your own helpless estate.
And remember your new life in Christ,
that holy blood spilled did create.
He's ready to empower you,
he's sufficient to help you embrace.
He's good, he's trustworthy, he's wise,
to redeem when you fall on your face.
Press into him on your hardest days,
let his word and Spirit in you dwell.
Though the night may seem to tarry,
the morning of your soul says it is well.

Ponder

Jesus endured the cross for the joy set before him, and that joy was seeing
you forgiven, cleansed, and healed. Similarly, parenting is a context to carry
your cross as you follow Jesus. It is often hard and sacrificial. What are some
of the joys God has set before you to help you endure?

Stay

Resolve to confess your sins and struggles more often to your children—
this is one of the most Christ-exalting things you can do for them. Con-
sider Ken Sande's "Seven A's of Confession" from his book, *The Peacemaker*.
(1) Avoid "If, But, or Maybe"; (2) Address Everyone Involved; (3) Admit

Specifically; (4) Acknowledge the Hurt; (5) Accept the Consequences; (6) Alter Your Behavior; (7) Ask for Forgiveness

Pray

Psalm 51:17: "The sacrifices of God are a broken spirit; a broken and contrite heart, O God, you will not despise."

Psalm 61:1–4: "Hear my cry, O God, listen to my prayer; from the end of the earth I call to you when my heart is faint. Lead me to the rock that is higher than I, for you have been my refuge, a strong tower against the enemy. Let me dwell in your tent forever! Let me take refuge under the shelter of your wings!"

1 Timothy 1:12–16: "I thank him who has given me strength, Christ Jesus our Lord, because he judged me faithful, appointing me to his service, though formerly I was a blasphemer, persecutor, and insolent opponent. But I received mercy because I had acted ignorantly in unbelief, and the grace of our Lord overflowed for me with the faith and love that are in Christ Jesus. The saying is trustworthy and deserving of full acceptance, that Christ Jesus came into the world to save sinners, of whom I am the foremost. But I received mercy for this reason, that in me, as the foremost, Jesus Christ might display his perfect patience as an example to those who were to believe in him for eternal life."

23. LOVE CALMS THE CHAOS

Trust in the Lord and do good,
wait for the LORD and keep his way.
Dwell in the land and befriend faithfulness,
guard your heart and what you say.
Though your heart may be throbbing,
and you feel your strength may fail.
Wait for the LORD and be patient,
his reprieve from this will prevail.
Watch what you post, watch how you speak,
and watch how you judge another.
Hearts are fickle and easily slip,
so be good to your sister and brother.
For perhaps the Lord shall not tarry,
and peace may resume in a flash.
And when you look back on your response,
were you filled with peace or were you crass?
Did you charitably relate to your neighbor,
did you seek to understand?
Or were you fired up, harsh, unkind,
and did you push away a friend?
The mouth of the righteous utters wisdom,
the law of his God is in his heart.
Even a fool is considered wise,
when he closes his mouth before he starts.
The simple believe everything,
but the prudent give it a second thought.
A tranquil heart brings life,
and he who is slow to anger will not be distraught.
Let your life be worthy of the gospel,
on other people and their words do not stew.
Set your minds on things above,
bear with others as God bears with you.
Do not forget compassionate hearts,
humility, patience, being meek.
Putting on love when we're tempted to fret,
thankful hearts change the words that we speak.

For Satan loves to stoke division,
relational conflict is a pot he delights to stir.
Fight him with acts of love,
standing together and being mature.
Continue steadfastly in prayer,
guard your heart as feelings swell.
Walk in wisdom, redeem the time,
love your difficult neighbor well.
And when your anger rises,
and a critical spirit grows.
Cast your burdens onto Christ,
for these temptations he surely knows.
Run to him and he will help,
he is pleased to answer such a cry.
Let's live in peace with one another,
and calm the chaos with the love he supplies.

Ponder

In Genesis 1:2–3, God brings order out of chaos. Think about how this was an act of love and wisdom. How it served the created world, including human beings. Then think about how God has calmed (or will calm) the chaos in your life through the love and wisdom of Jesus Christ.

Stay

When stress comes to your home, your office, your church, or your heart, how do you typically respond? Write down a few of your "go to" methods of dealing with stress and chaos. Now evaluate whether they are from God or from the world, the flesh, and the devil.

Pray

Psalm 34:14: "Turn away from evil and do good; seek peace and pursue it."

Matthew 24:12: "And because lawlessness will be increased, the love of many will grow cold. But the one who endures to the end will be saved."

Colossians 3:14–15: "And above all these put on love, which binds everything together in perfect harmony. And let the peace of Christ rule in your hearts, to which indeed you were called in one body. And be thankful."

24. MORNING PRAYER

Before the sunlight of the day,
gleams in its glory above.
I sit and pray to give my heart,
to my Father in heaven that I love.
Lord, take my day and all my plans,
let me give them all to you.
Use my time, talents, and hands,
to bring you glory that is due.
Keep my heart with vigilance,
let springs of life pour out.
Let Jesus and his atoning work,
be my fuel this day throughout.
And when between my morning prayer,
and how I live a gap appears.
Instead of pulling away my Savior,
it's in these moments you draw near.
Keep me dependent, give me joy,
today may your truth I embrace.
Give me your goodness as my ally,
your compassion, mercy, and grace.

Ponder

Take a moment to be amazed that out of billions of sinners, God chose you, called you, saved you, and will soon glorify you.

Stay

God is both a morning person and a night owl. How can you build talking with him in the morning and evening into the rhythm of your day?

Pray

Psalm 90:14: "Satisfy us in the morning with your steadfast love, that we may rejoice and be glad all our days."

Psalm 121:2–4: "My help comes from the LORD, the Maker of heaven and earth. He will not let your foot slip—he who watches over you will not slumber; indeed, he who watches over Israel will neither slumber nor sleep." (NIV)

Matthew 6:9–13:

"Pray then like this:
Our Father in heaven,
hallowed be your name.
Your kingdom come,
your will be done,
on earth as it is in heaven.
Give us this day our daily bread,
and forgive us our debts,
as we also have forgiven our debtors.
And lead us not into temptation,
but deliver us from evil."

25. RECOGNITION

I want to be somebody,
I want glory, to be seen.
I pine after encouraging words,
I won't settle for in between.
To prove myself as worthy,
in what I do or places I go.
My identity in my children,
or my work, or what I know.
Boasting in my marriage,
obsessing about my charm.
Or perhaps it's my looks,
my body shape or my arms.
The money I make, the house I own,
or perhaps my treasure is in being frugal.
The thrill I get to order water,
instead of paying for a drink; is my approval.
Proving how much wisdom I have,
how much in the know I seem to be.
I know all the news, every current event,
if you have questions, of course ask me.
My intellect, my degree, my book,
my accomplishments in my career.
The charisma I have with people,
or how much of my time I volunteer.
Recognition, recognition,
the cry of meaning in my life.
I want to be a somebody,
to be acknowledged brings delight.
Recognition recognition,
People noticing quenches my thirst.
Validation is my trophy,
I need to say this or I'll burst.
What is it for you this season,
the deeper reason you seek to be known?
What recognition are you not receiving
one that makes you fret and feel alone?

Let me bring you hope and cheer,
for as you see, recognition quests will fail.
And all the glory that you desire,
will in the end your hopes derail.
But there is someone near your heart,
who sees and who remembers you.
Whose love has set you apart for more,
than any person or praise can do.
The one who laid down his rights,
all glory was his in creation making.
But instead of glory now,
suffering first was his undertaking.
He associated with lowliness,
weakness, and apparent defeat.
He did not grasp after accolades,
submitting to the Father he was complete.
Out of all the souls that ever lived,
Jesus Christ deserved recognition.
Moral purity and perfection,
intelligence and clarity his ammunition.
Character impeccable,
wisdom in the flesh.
Knowledge, power, in the know,
his friendship passed all tests.
Experience and expertise,
the resume of the perfect man.
Owner of heaven and earth,
who before him could rightly stand?
And how did humanity respond to him,
did they bow, did they stand in awe?
Did they seek to lean in closer,
to learn from and trust in the one they saw?
No, they called him a liar,
a blasphemer, in league with the evil one.
They hated him, rejected him,
God's only begotten Son.
Tortured him, belittled him,
forcing a cross as his shoulders bled.

The hands and hearts of those he created,
empowered to beat and kill him instead.
And do you think if our Savior,
carried such a smite.
That a servant is better than his master,
and your recognition will bring you life?
Not from the east or from the west,
but from God who ordains our cup.
It is God who puts down one,
and it is God who lifts another up.
And Jesus laid down his life,
of his own accord and will.
So that he could take it up again,
and recognize you to the full.
In the rearview mirror of your life,
seeing your accomplishments and their beauty.
Pray and hope that you will say,
I am an unworthy servant, I have done what was my duty.
For one day all your labors,
in obscurity or in the limelight.
Will be cast down at Jesus' feet,
as crowns that belong to him by rite.
For what do you have that you did not receive,
you have nothing that isn't from his hand.
So use it for his glory and praise,
your Savior sees and he understands.
One day you'll realize it was all for him,
when you touch his wounds and see his face.
And on that day all recognition,
will settle in to its proper place.

Ponder

God's love is unconditional, to the uttermost, and unending. Human love is often conditional, half-hearted, and fleeting. How does that free you from worrying so much about what people think of you?

Stay

In what area of life do you crave approval or recognition most? (Hint: it will be something you think about a lot, are willing to sin to get, and are angry or despairing when you don't). Take some time to talk to God about it this week.

Pray

Psalm 49:16: "Be not afraid when a man becomes rich, when the glory of his house increases. For when he dies he will carry nothing away; his glory will not go down after him. For though, while he lives, he counts himself blessed—and though you get praise when you do well for yourself—his soul will go to the generation of his fathers, who will never again see light."

Matthew 6:3–4: "But when you give to the needy, do not let your left hand know what your right hand is doing, so that your giving may be in secret. And your Father who sees in secret will reward you."

John 13:1: "It was just before the Passover Festival. Jesus knew that the hour had come for him to leave this world and go to the Father. Having loved his own who were in the world, he loved them to the end." (NIV)

26. BATTLING THE BAD ANGER

In our broken world,
so much to fill our minds.
Many reasons to be angry,
things gone wrong, not hard to find.
God also gets angry,
and hates wrong in this life.
But in our fleshly nature,
anger goes sideways and not right.
We want something good,
but it's far away from reach.
Respect, power, affirmation,
convenience, comfort, peace.
Maybe we just want intimacy,
money, safety, help, or pleasure.
But these desires grow too big,
and become our heart's treasure.
"My will be done, My kingdom come,"
is the deeper outburst that we cry.
And we blow up, gossip, complain,
hold a grudge or don't reply.
We get even, we get bitter,
cynical, hostile, placing blame.
Our neighbor's actions irritate us,
a critical spirit starts to reign.
"They are so inconsistent,
they are all over the place."
"They are selfish, they are foolish,
so sensitive, always rude and late."
And what else is a critical spirit,
but finding fault in everyone?
We assume the role of God,
and with our words they're undone.
Harsh, often self-righteous,
my opinion put forth as what's true.
All the while we're forgetting,
in our heart the sins that brew.

There is a place for making judgements,
to discern and to evaluate.
But it is much more redemptive,
when driven by love and faith.
For if you, O LORD, should mark my iniquities,
O LORD who could stand?
And yet I am so quick to be critical,
have I even sought to understand?
My heart is deceitful above all things,
and oh so desperately sick and blind.
My biggest problem is not "out there,"
it is the log in my eye I've yet to find.
And as I am humbled by my sin,
my weakness and need for the Lord.
Constructively responding to wrongs,
is a business I can now afford.
Enter patience, slow to anger,
this is God's world, it's his throne.
All the people that I criticize,
are in a process of their own.
Enter mercy, trying to make it right,
is there is anything I can do?
Let mercy replace critique,
for God extended such to you.
Enter forgiveness to the wrongs we feel,
absorbing the hurt, letting peace abound.
Overcoming evil with good,
not insisting now justice be found.
Enter confrontation when called for,
not giving in to rant or rave.
For your loving confrontation,
may be the correction that may save.
The opposite of sinful anger and critique,
is not ignoring what is truly wrong.
It can be redemptive, it can be godly,
tuning our heart to a better song.
The song of a Savior,
that endured our hateful rage.

The anger in our hearts,
is why he came to save.
"Crucify him, crucify him,"
would have been our own reply.
Every outburst and angry thought,
is why Jesus had to die.
But thank God when we trust in Christ,
he gives us grace to overcome.
Grace to redeem our anger,
because we come by blood of the Son.

Ponder

God is the most angry person in the Bible. Why is that? Where do we find Jesus getting angry in the gospels?

Stay

What typically provokes you to anger? How does this reveal a desire to be in control or to be right? What would putting on fruit of the Spirit in those moments look like? Be specific.

Pray

Psalm 4:4: "Be angry, and do not sin; ponder in your own hearts on your beds, and be silent."

Ecclesiastes 7:9: "Be not quick in your spirit to become angry, for anger lodges in the heart of fools."

Galatians 5:22–25: "But the fruit of the Spirit is love, joy, peace, patience, kindness, goodness, faithfulness, gentleness, self-control; against such things there is no law. And those who belong to Christ Jesus have crucified the flesh with its passions and desires. If we live by the Spirit, let us also keep in step with the Spirit."

27. SOWING TEARS, REAPING JOY

"I don't know why I'm crying Mommy,"
as tears rolled down her cheeks.
Struggling, not knowing why,
a common occurrence on some weeks.
And as I looked into her eyes,
reflecting back to me.
Were the tears I often cry,
and the same confusing plea.
Lord, I know some cries are anger,
some cries are my frustration.
But as I live another day,
I see a world of chaos and vexation.
Tears for evil, tears for corruption,
salty tears for those who hurt.
Hatred, hypocrisy, loss, futility,
tears fill my pillow and my shirt.
And all my tears are pointing,
to a world that's gone astray.
Every drop that streams my face,
cries it's not suppose to be this way.
So do I hide my emotions,
stuff them deep inside?
Or dump an outburst of debris,
on every person that I find?
No, I see a better path,
to plant my tears instead.
In the depths of my being and presence of God,
I pray in safety to the godhead.
Even when I don't see,
what God is up to here.
My understanding limited,
yet in his word he draws me near.
He knows my desperation,
it is safe to cry aloud.
As I let my prayers be planted,
and my will to him is bowed.

Those who sow in tears,
with shouts of joy shall reap.
If my trust be found in Jesus,
this is a promise I can keep.
He who goes out weeping,
bearing seed for sowing.
Shall come home bringing sheaves with him,
and his shouts of joy be overflowing.
For there stands a man of sorrows,
who tasted these same tears.
Jesus abandoned in my place,
so to the Father I can draw near.
The Lord my chosen portion,
you who hold my lot.
I have a beautiful inheritance,
because I have been bought.
By the precious blood of Christ,
my flesh shall dwell secure.
Knowing I shall not be forsaken,
these salty tears I can endure.
So with simple words and compassion,
I hold my child's hand and pray.
Knowing her tears that flow like mine,
will by our Savior be wiped away.
I encourage her to sow them,
to the One who took her place.
The tears my Jesus tasted,
so his comfort I could embrace.
Tears are filled with complexities,
that only God can know.
So sow your tears to him,
and his harvest he will show.
Restoring, confirming, establishing,
strengthening you with greater hope.
There is a river of gladness coming,
and my tears will topple down its slope.
Because he is at our right hand,
we shall not be shaken from his graces.

The path of life, the fullness of joy,
the lines have fallen for me in pleasant places.

Ponder

God wonderfully promises to keep track of each of your tears and sorrows
(Ps 56:8). As sweet as that is, it gets better. He has acted in history to make
sure a day is coming when each sadness is not only destroyed but replaced
by a reciprocal joy (Rev 21). Let that good news settle into your spirit.

Stay

For the Christian, there is always light at the end of the tunnel. Where can
you focus more on the good that is coming in heaven and Jesus' return than
on the bad that is happening now?

Pray

Psalm 42:5–6: "Why are you cast down, O my soul, and why are you in
turmoil within me? Hope in God; for I shall again praise him, my salvation
and my God."

Psalm 126:5–6: "Those who sow in tears shall reap with shouts of joy! He
who goes out weeping, bearing the seed for sowing, shall come home with
shouts of joy, bringing his sheaves with him."

Revelation 3:11–12: "I am coming soon. Hold fast what you have, so that
no one may seize your crown. The one who conquers, I will make him a
pillar in the temple of my God. Never shall he go out of it, and I will write
on him the name of my God, and the name of the city of my God, the new
Jerusalem, which comes down from my God out of heaven, and my own
new name."

28. STAY IN YOUR CIRCLE

So many needs, so much to do,
where do I even begin?
Good choices, decisions to make,
which is the direction for me to go in?
Paralysis by analysis,
how do I spend my time?
When so many calls beckon me,
and for my attention pine.
Wisdom helps us step back,
ponder, pause, and think.
What has God called me to,
and what can I leave on the brink?
Stay in my first concentric circle,
who is in front of me now and here?
Who is present in flesh and blood,
and what callings has God made clear?
Face to face, in person,
serving those in proximity.
My neighbors all around,
need good works flowing from me.
Scrolling and media may have their place,
keeping in touch with those from afar.
But priority given to our sphere,
the town we live and where we are.
We are limited, we are finite,
we cannot be everywhere all the time.
Our Savior came to the earth,
and handled this just fine.
He could have been everywhere,
doing good in every place.
But in his frail humanity,
he was limited by time and space.
Most of his time spent,
with twelve normal guys he loved.
Building into them and teaching them,
content to do the Father's will above.

God has likewise given us,
a place to serve, a place to pursue.
Your family, friends, acquaintances,
neighbors that need all of you.
Sometimes we have to say no,
to opportunities calling our name.
And chose deeper over wider,
deep sea diving becoming our aim.
Who is it you need to stay with,
in love build into, pursue, and enclose?
Perhaps in looking out too wide,
you've missed what's in front of your nose.
Stay in your circle, do simple things well,
what needs are in front of you?
With excellence walk in the callings he's given,
And God will give grace as you do.

Ponder

How much can you really control? What outcomes can you truly guarantee?
Make a list of the things you worry about that are actually and ultimately
in God's hands.

Stay

Where do you feel like not enough butter scraped over too much bread?
That is, where are you trying to exceed the good limitations of your hu-
manity? Usually, it looks like chasing the ability to be everywhere, to know
everything, or to do everything. As the Spirit leads, repent of that desire
and rest in God's love, wisdom, and sovereignty.

Pray

Mark 1:35–37: "And rising very early in the morning, while it was still dark,
he departed and went out to a desolate place, and there he prayed. And

Simon and those who were with him searched for him, and they found him and said to him, "Everyone is looking for you."

Galatians 6:10: "So then, as we have opportunity, let us do good to everyone, and especially to those who are of the household of faith."

Ephesians 5:15–17: "Look carefully then how you walk, not as unwise but as wise, making the best use of the time, because the days are evil. Therefore do not be foolish, but understand what the will of the Lord is."

29. BE AT PEACE

Is there someone on your mind
that rolls around in there?
She did this to me, how could he?
It simply is not fair.
Stewing in your anger
your mind keeps hitting replay.
As you think of all the sassy things,
if you had the gall you'd say.
This thing they do annoys me,
this past hurt I can't let go.
You say to just forgive them?
but how do I let *that* go?
Relationships are tricky,
two impure people side by side.
Inevitably you'll be hurt,
sin and selfishness cannot hide.
Each of us has felt it,
anger, control, bitterness, greed.
Jealousy, envy, pride,
is what all our conflicts breed.
But there's a hope that is stronger,
and can free us from this snare.
Of being controlled by another,
when we let bitterness linger there.
A hope of grace and rescue,
from ourselves and what we let stew.
We can put to death this trap,
and let peace and love ensue.
Keep your heart with vigilance,
for from it flow springs of life.
We all have hearts that need to change,
if any relationship be made right.
The Giver of grace is willing,
he hears your whisper and your shout.
And by his Spirit's power,
he can change you from the inside out.

The fear of the Lord is a fountain of life,
none who run to this fountain will thirst.
For we will walk in newness of life,
because Christ was raised to glory first.
If he can conquer sin and death,
and reign and rule at God's right hand.
Then there is no relationship,
that is too hard for his command.
Whatever is true, whatever is lovely,
whatever is just and pure.
Our God has made a way for peace,
as we humble ourselves, he'll restore.
Our hope is in the Savior,
who has perfectly related to all.
And because he's walked our trials,
he thinks our conflicts no thing small.
Freedom is found in his love,
and in his lavish grace we stand.
As we extend this grace to friends,
with a generous and open hand.
Let compassion rule the day,
humility, meekness, patience, prayer too.
Look for the good in this person,
be at peace as much as depends on you.
In Christ we have a hope,
built on his beautiful name.
An inheritance of glory,
where none will be put to shame.
And one day when we get there,
oh how enlightened our hearts will be.
All the wrestling with each other,
a blip on the radar of eternity.

Ponder

Read Romans 5:6–11. Paul uses the words, *weak, ungodly, sinners, wrath of God,* and *enemies* to describe our relationship with God prior to meeting

Jesus. He uses the words, *Christ died for, God shows his love, justified by his blood, saved by him, reconciled to God,* and *rejoice* to describe God's initiative to restore our relationship with him. Take time to meditate on each contrast; the before and after of being reconciled to your Creator.

Stay

Consider any past or present relationships where there is tension. What does God's word call you to do? How does the nature of the gospel renew your thinking and empower your behavior in these relationships?

Pray

Nehemiah 9:17: "They refused to obey and were not mindful of the wonders that you performed among them, but they stiffened their neck and appointed a leader to return to their slavery in Egypt. But you are a God ready to forgive, gracious and merciful, slow to anger and abounding in steadfast love, and did not forsake them."

Ephesians 4:31–32: "Let all bitterness and wrath and anger and clamor and slander be put away from you, along with all malice. Be kind to one another, tenderhearted, forgiving one another, as God in Christ forgave you."

2 Corinthians 5:18–19: "All this is from God, who through Christ reconciled us to himself and gave us the ministry of reconciliation; that is, in Christ God was reconciling the world to himself, not counting their trespasses against them, and entrusting to us the message of reconciliation."

30. TAMING THE TONGUE

The tongue, such a small member,
yet boasts of things so great.
How I use my words,
can destroy, heal, or inspire faith.
The tongue is a fire,
a world of unrighteousness set.
No human being can tame the tongue,
we curse others and we forget.
That a harvest of righteousness is sown,
in peace by those who make peace.
So my gossip and my slander,
do not serve anyone in the least.
Gossip is spreading unfavorable,
information even if it's true.
Slander is destroying a reputation,
a piece of news we easily misconstrue.
When we ascribe wrong motives,
even when inside a heart we can't see.
We assume, we fill in the blanks,
and lose all sense of charity.
Usually it's because we're upset,
feel slighted, angry, and hurt.
It feels so good to vent our words,
so it's gossip and slander that we blurt.
We make someone appear more sinful,
blow out of proportion the person they are.
We exaggerate their faults,
and when we do this it leaves a scar.
Because those who hear our words,
now perceive this person as so.
The words that left my mouth,
I cannot take back as they go.
How can I avoid this plague,
this joyless, fruitless endeavor?
Especially when I feel justified,
for the hurt that I've had to weather?

First, have I sought to reconcile,
as much as depends on me made peace?
Moved towards a conversation with them,
prayed that my bitterness would decrease.
Have I sought to understand,
do I know the full story, have I asked?
Usually it's easier to slander and gossip,
over pursuing godly peacemaking tasks.
Have I pondered the way that is blameless,
walked with integrity in my speech?
Knowing that what comes out of my mouth,
comes from my heart that I need to reach.
Reciting gospel truth that God the Father,
sent his only begotten Son.
I was just like the person I slander,
he died for me the unrighteous one.
If I believe Christ died for my sins,
I believe also the cross has declared.
I am a sinner, a wretch, a fool,
filled with countless sins I'm unaware.
A humble response will see my state,
and fall desperately on my knees.
Before I open my mouth about others,
"Lord thank you" for your grace towards me.
He who is forgiven little loves little,
but he who sees his own sin love abounds.
And corrupting talk will be far from his lips,
and only words that build up will be found.
Is it kind? Is it necessary?
Does it give grace to those who hear?
Let all bitterness, wrath, anger and slander,
be put away from you; it brings no cheer.
Be kind to one another, tenderhearted,
forgiving one another today.
As God in Christ forgave you,
and you'll put his power on display.
Maybe there is someone today,
you need to call to confess and inquire.

Understand what they were thinking,
bringing humility instead of fire.
Go to them, pursue them, reconcile,
be free of their control over you.
Confess all your struggles,
Jesus will help, he's tried and true.

Ponder

Why is it that we would never want someone to gossip about us or slander our character, but can find it so easy (and pleasurable) to do it to others?

Stay

How much of your "kitchen talk" is grateful and encouraging? How much is venting your spirit about the mistakes and flaws of others? Ask a godly friend or spouse to give their honest assessment of the content of your speech.

Pray

Proverbs 11:13: "Whoever goes about slandering reveals secrets, but he who is trustworthy in spirit keeps a thing covered."

James 3:6, 9: "And the tongue is a fire, a world of unrighteousness. The tongue is set among our members, straining the whole body . . . With it we bless our Lord and Father, and with it we curse people who are made in the likeness of God."

Ephesians 4:29: "Let no corrupting talk come out of your mouths, but only such as is good for building up, as fits the occasion, that it may give grace to those who hear."

31. SWORDS DOWN, EYES UP

I'm living with you all the time,
I see you at your worst and best.
Your habits, idiosyncrasies,
are endearing; I feel blessed.
Some days I cherish you,
on those days it's my joy and delight.
On other days you annoy me,
I'm contentious and I fight.
You don't give me what I want,
so I quarrel, covet, and demand.
My passions are at war within,
this struggle hard to understand.
On simpler occasions it works out,
and peace and calmness reign.
At other times my heart is hardened,
and I refuse to give up my terrain.
Sulking, despairing, seething,
letting the anger grow beneath.
It seems the person closest to me,
knows how to cut me deep.
So I go to bed angry,
or I justify my part.
I say such unkind words,
my mouth overflowing with my heart.
What does it take in these moments,
in these seasons, on those days?

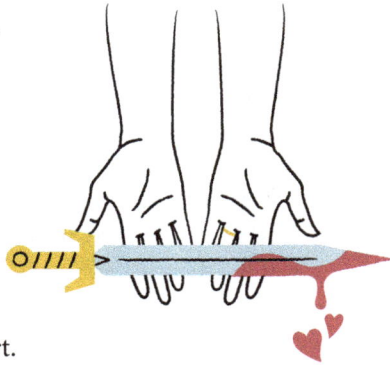

Only the grace of God,
can keep a hardened heart at bay.
The sacrifice God desires,
is a heart broken and contrite.
A bruise reed he will not break,
nor quench a burning wick in spite.
Humble yourself under his mighty hand,
at the proper time you may be exalted.
Cast your burdens on him,

on his promises he's never defaulted.
Remember the vows keep you,
the promises you've made.
Whatever you thought you signed up for,
this is the hand he graciously gave.
How easy it is to love someone,
when lovable and endearing they are.
Loving you when you're ugly,
difficult, and sinful is harder by far.
Yet I know the Incarnate Christ,
the perfect, spotless, righteous lamb.
Who left the glories of heaven,
to heal this marriage I can't understand.
Perhaps for a good person,
one would dare even to die.
But perfect Jesus breathed his last,
as I mocked and spit in his eye.
While we were still sinners,
not after we made ourselves clean.
While I was foolish, disobedient, a slave to my pleasure,
Jesus came to make pure what was obscene.
If this same Jesus enduring,
a shameful and painful death on a cross.
Living a life of obedience, serving,
and suffering at such a cost.
Could look upon me with compassion,
mercy, grace, forgiveness, and delight.
What could I possibly have to gain,
from holding firmly to being right?
Say, "I'm sorry, I was wrong,
Please forgive me my dear."
Pray and ask him for his help,
and he will make his truth more clear.
Seek out friends for counsel,
healing and restoring are in his realm.
Admitting your sins and weaknesses,
can be the remedy for the overwhelmed.
It's worth it to fight for your marriage,

it's worth it to fight till the end.
Commitment a fleeting virtue,
moving on; the world's message to send.
What God has brought together,
let no one separate.
One flesh, a serious union,
there can be joy; it's not too late.
God is sufficient, God is near,
God is more powerful than you can conceive.
Seek the Lord while he can be found,
his ways can be trusted when you believe.
And in the thick of conflict,
remember the lengths he's taken.
To ensure you are safe in him,
and that you'll never be forsaken.
He who is forgiven little,
has little to love in their soul.
But the one who has been forgiven much,
can help others become whole.

Ponder

Read James 4:1–10. How does this make sense of marriage conflict and give you hope for real change?

Stay

When was the last time you invited a friend or couple to speak into your marriage? Where you shared your joys, confessed your sins, admitted your fears, and asked for prayer? If it's been a while, consider reaching out to someone this week.

Pray

Exodus 34:6–7: "The LORD passed in front of Moses, calling out, 'Yahweh! The LORD! The God of compassion and mercy! I am slow to anger and filled with unfailing love and faithfulness. I lavish unfailing love to a thousand generations. I forgive iniquity, rebellion, and sin."(NLT)

Psalm 147:3: "He heals the brokenhearted and binds up their wounds."

Colossians 3:12–13: "Put on then, as God's chosen ones, holy and beloved, compassionate hearts, kindness, humility, meekness, and patience, bearing with one another and, if one has a complaint against another, forgiving each other; as the Lord has forgiven you, so you also must forgive."

32. THE LITTLE THINGS

When my heart is overwhelmed,
lead me to the rock that is high.
Jesus hear my every plea,
my every tear and cry.
This world is not as it should be,
since the fall it has been broken.
Thank God for the hope we have,
in your Word, God, you have spoken.
Quiet trust, giving my burdens to you,
my anxious heart and all my frets.
For you are making all things new,
Jesus you have conquered sin and death.
And as we wait for this sorrowful world,
to instead by joy be driven.
May it please you God in heaven,
to enjoy the little pleasures you've given.
A little child's fingers,
intertwined with my own.
A sunset, a good meal,
time to think and time alone.
Friendship, family, belly laughs,
a hug, a phone call, an embrace.
Reconciling and making peace,
letting all bitterness be erased.
A gentle breeze on a hot day,
finding something that you've lost.
Receiving an act of kindness,
or sacrificial love at such a cost.
An encouraging note from a friend,
a timely word you needed to hear.
Reprieve from a lingering sickness,
finally conquering that terrible fear.
Your car working and running,
gas in your car, food on your table.
A job you get to work hard at,
producing, subduing, and stable.

A snuggle, a hug, or a picture,
from your precious little child.
Watching them when they sleep,
laughing when they go quirky wild.
A song that reaches deep into your soul,
while tears stream down your face.
Reminding you of someone you love,
or a different time and better place.
The little things are everywhere,
if we are wise enough to see.
One day, one hour, one moment,
is where we need to be.
Merciful, and gracious,
steadfast love his work of art.
All the little things,
are a window to God's heart.

Ponder

Think about the places you spend most of your time in. Think about the people you spend most of your time with. What are some of the small gifts, the extras, God has given in them that you might often overlook?

Stay

Take a moment in the morning, midday, and evening to thank God for the ordinary gifts of the day. Push your mind to notice the seemingly insignificant, the assumed and expected blessings the Father fills your life with every day.

Pray

Ephesians 5:20: ". . . giving thanks always and for everything to God the Father in the name of our Lord Jesus Christ. . ."

Ecclesiastes 5:18: "Behold, what I have seen to be good and fitting is to eat and drink and find enjoyment in all the toil with which one toils under the sun the few days of his life that God has given him, for this is his lot."

Acts 17:25: " . . . since he himself gives to all mankind life and breath and everything."

33. BROKEN CISTERNS

Have I hewed out cisterns,
that no water could ever hold?
Forsaken the God whom I love,
replaced the one I'm meant to behold?
For every time I desire glory,
or seek after that which profits not.
It fills me for a moment,
but then that cistern starts to rot.
The lie that lures me in,
whispering my heart will get its fill.
Instead just leaves me empty,
after such a momentary thrill.
And in a time of confusion,
when stress surrounds on every side.
We tend to crave a quick relief,
in things that take us by surprise.
As the suffering that you feel,
squeezes the lemon of your life.
Part of the squeezing does reveal,
a sour heart that stirs with strife.
Seeking deeper pleasures,
comfort, quiet, ambition, and peace.
Power, prestige, affirmation,
order, control, success, to say the least.
Good things in themselves,
but how and where we place them is all wrong.
Because we make them gods we serve,
we fail to hear the true God's song.
When we sin to get what we want,
or we sin when it's out of our grasp.
We know we love it far too much,
our response a warning light on the dash.
Waking us up to a deeper need,
that is brewing in the recess of our core.
We have misplaced our affections,
and forgotten God gives so much more.

Nothing on this earth can satisfy,
even if the whole world we should gain.
Perfect comfort, perfect savings,
perfect life goals, all in vain.
If we gain our hopes and dreams,
and have not Jesus as our joy.
Then everything we've ever gained,
will in the end our heart destroy.
Our idols don't deliver,
they make promises they can't keep.
They never truly satisfy,
smooth like honey but cut so deep.
So there is freedom when we find,
the sour drippings of our heart.
For when we know the root of sin,
it gives our soul a place to start.
The resources and the promises,
are found in God's great book.
The gospel hope that we cling to,
our only solid place of rest to look.
If we say that we have sinned,
and confess our sins, he'll hear.
He is faithful and just to forgive us,
and cleanse us from the unrighteousness we fear.
And as we are squeezed of our sin,
from the one whose hand loves us so.
Lean and abide in his faithfulness,
walk in the light of grace he'll bestow.
For we have an advocate with the Father,
Jesus Christ the righteous one.
He is the propitiation for our sins,
when we know him from idols we'll run.
So don't be defeated by your sin,
leaking out of your heart everyday.
This revelation leads to abiding,
knowing him leads to walking his same way.
The Holy Spirit is in the business,
of bringing out the vile.

But for every one look at your sin,
keep your eyes on Christ awhile.
And as the Spirit gets to work,
he fills your life with victory.
As you transform from the inside,
into the person God meant you to be.

Ponder

An idol can be anything and has been everything. Something (or some-one) that promises freedom, security, meaning, or fulfillment but can never provide it (because it isn't God). Idols demand that we love, trust, and obey them . . . and then enslave us. What are some attractive idols in our culture today? (see Acts 17:16)

Stay

How does the gospel provide the *approval* an idol cannot? How does the gospel provide the *freedom* an idol cannot? How does the gospel provide the *security* an idol cannot?

Pray

Jeremiah 2:11–13: " . . . But my people have changed their glory for that which does not profit. Be appalled, O heavens, at this; be shocked, be utterly desolate, declares the LORD, for my people have committed two evils: they have forsaken me, the fountain of living waters, and hewed out cisterns for themselves, broken cisterns that can hold no water."

1 Peter 3:18: "For Christ also suffered once for sins, the righteous for the unrighteous, that he might bring us to God, being put to death in the flesh but made alive in the spirit..."

2 Peter 1:3–4: "His divine power has granted to us all things that pertain to life and godliness, through the knowledge of him who called us to his

own glory and excellence, by which he has granted to us his precious and very great promises, so that through them you may become partakers of the divine nature, having escaped from the corruption that is in the world because of sinful desire."

34. LOVING ORDER OR LOVING OTHERS?

A question I have often pondered,
or other parents share with me.
How do you balance a clean house,
with children's messy tendencies?
Where is the line,
how much do I fuss?
Do I follow them around and clean,
do I let them run amuck?
Visual chaos is a real thing,
for many parents it brings stress.
Depending on the way God's made you,
sometimes it's hard to leave a mess.
Every time I try to clean a room,
enter my little tornadoes to swirl about.
Undoing all my hard work,
the order I created completely crossed out.
Some categories to think in,
that may help to clear our mind.
First, is this a child's weakness,
or their sin that I seem to find?
Children are just messy,
they touch, they undo, they destroy.
But weakness is not sin,
it is what makes a human girl or boy.
Weakness is the spilled milk on the table,
pictures on walls with makeup when they're 3.
Cutting their hair because it annoys them,
trying to shave just like their Daddy.
Taking out toys and then walking away,
falling down stairs, making a hole in the wall.
Cutting the flowers you've worked hard to grow,
to give them as gifts to the sister they know.
Their weaknesses often inconvenience us,
the cleanup, the hassle, the sweat.
But underneath the chaos an opportunity,
for our selfishness to be reset.

Second the spirit in which we teach,
about picking up and cleaning to start.
Matters to God, matters to them,
since when has nagging ever changed a heart?
As we teach them how to clean,
for order and tidiness is good.
Teach them with a lighter heart,
how to be part of a family as they should.
Yes, they need to learn chores,
as they get older the more this should be.
But stressing about a messy house,
makes everything all about me.
What do I want etched in their memory,
a parent who fumes and reams?
Because they interrupted,
the house I desire to always be clean?
Is my house a museum of my idols,
do not touch, do not taste, bow down.
To all of the ways I prefer,
a world where no playing is found?
Messes may be imagination,
creativity, experiments, pretend.
Do my children feel loved as they play,
is this the clear message I send?
Letting it go, watching them have fun,
keeping "stuff" in it's proper place.
There will always be time for cleaning,
but moments with children cannot be replaced.
Teach them to clean up, yes,
to be unselfish, good stewards a must.
But remember the deposit you're making,
is less about clean than of trust.
Trusting you love them more than your stuff,
more than organization and cleanly floors.
Sit with, read, love and snuggle them,
this is time your heart can afford.
For if your kids were gone,
and your home could be just so.

Everything in its proper place,
you wouldn't have any room to grow.

Ponder

In creation God brings order to chaos. He takes what is formless and void and shapes it toward beauty. And yet, it is only after creating human beings made in his image and likeness that he pronounces creation, "very good." Meditate on the gifts you experience in your relationship with God as an image-bearer in comparison to animals, plants, and the rest of creation.

Stay

How would those who know you best answer the question, "Are they more interested in projects or people?" How might God want to change the way you relate to tasks vs quality and quantity time with people?

Pray

Proverbs 21: 2–3: "Every way of a man is right in his own eyes, but the LORD weighs the heart. To do righteousness and justice is more acceptable to the LORD than sacrifice."

Mark 12:33: "And to love him with all the heart and with all the understanding and with all the strength, and to love one's neighbor as oneself, is much more than all whole burnt offerings and sacrifices."

Romans 14:17–19: "For the kingdom of God is not a matter of eating and drinking but of righteousness and peace and joy in the Holy Spirit. Whoever thus serves Christ is acceptable to God and approved by men. So then let us pursue what makes for peace and for mutual upbuilding."

35. A PRAYER FOR MY LIMITS

Let me give all my failings to you,
resting in the One who sets it right.
Let me give all my fears and angst,
to the One in whom my soul delights.
Let me give all my victories also,
the little battles with the flesh I won.
By the Spirit and with his power,
if anything good, because of the Son.
Let me give the concerns of tomorrow,
to the One who is already there.
His sovereignty covers all times,
and my future is under his care.
Let me give him all people I carry,
on my heart heavy like a stone.
For the God whose wisdom is mighty,
can comfort, protect, and atone.
Let me rest tonight in my God,
he who does not slumber or sleep.
He protects my going out and coming in,
so I can close my eyes and rest deep.

Ponder

The Bible teaches that God has placed limits on us as created beings. For example, the need for love, laughter, food, sleep and protection. Consider how each limit is a gift to be received, not a problem to be solved. Each one designed by your Creator to draw you toward him. It is the feeling of having to do more in less time on your own that drives you away from him.

Stay

Make a list of stressors in your life. Pray that God would use the stress to bring about good but also protect you from relating to it with anxiety. Pray that he might give you grace to cast each stress onto him and be fully present in every situation. Pray that he would help you lose yourself in the good things (and works) he's prepared for you this week.

Pray

Psalm 111:10: "The fear of the LORD is the beginning of wisdom; all those who practice it have a good understanding. His praise endures forever!"

Psalm 127:1–2: "Unless the LORD builds the house, those who build it labor in vain. Unless the LORD watches over the city, the watchman stays awake in vain. It is in vain that you rise up early and go late to rest, eating the bread of anxious toil; for he gives to his beloved sleep."

John 10:9–11: "I am the door. If anyone enters by me, he will be saved and will go in and out and find pasture. The thief comes only to steal and kill and destroy. I came that they may have life and have it abundantly. I am the good shepherd. The good shepherd lays down his life for the sheep."

36. FRIENDSHIP

Because you are made in the image of God,
you need people and they need you.
A healthy evaluation of friendship,
might be a fruitful, relevant thing to pursue.
As you take time this week to think,
where have your relationships stood?
Do you often lay aside your preferences,
and consider serving others as you should?
Have people over projects,
been the normal rhythm of your life?
Or have you run to busyness,
and not dealt with bitter strife?
A friend loves, a friend stays,
a friend meets you where you are.
A friendship requires risk,
and can remain close even when far.
How about asking for forgiveness,
do you need to talk something through?
Is there someone that needs to hear,
a healing word from you?
Do you sit and wait for people to call,
or do you take courage and initiate?
Are you faithful to follow up and ask,
how you can help carry a weight?
And if you feel like a failure remember,
in Christ there is no condemnation left to hold.
Drawing near in full assurance of faith,
because of our high priest we can be bold.
Bold to be a friend that loves,
pursues, sacrifices, and stays.
Is not afraid to share their heart,
be real, go deep, and pray.
Because sustaining your deepest or longest friendship,
is the same Savior that one day you'll see.
He shows us how to be a friend,
with great compassion, depth, and mastery.

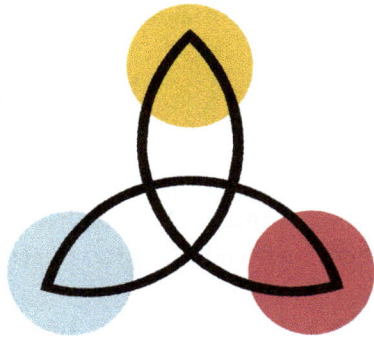

In every friendship he grants,
there is a tuning of the orchestra of your soul.
Which will soon give way to a heavenly symphony,
of fellowship and love that will make us whole.

Ponder

The Father, the Son, and the Holy Spirit have lived as three distinct persons in perfect fellowship (or friendship, or oneness) for all eternity. How does that affect the value you place on friendship?

Stay

What are some friendships God has blessed you with? Have you told them recently how meaningful their friendship is? If not, write them a card this week.

Pray

Proverbs 18:24: "One who has unreliable friends soon comes to ruin, but there is a friend who sticks closer than a brother." (NIV)

John 17:11b: "Holy Father, keep them in your name, which you have given me, that they may be one, even as we are one."

James 1:17: "Every good gift and every perfect gift is from above, coming down from the Father of lights, with whom there is no variation or shadow due to change."

37. THORNY ROSES

How often have I stepped outside,
to enjoy fresh cut grass and its smell?
But did you know the grass is crying,
when it's cut the scent's a yell?
For all creation is groaning,
until from bondage it's set free.
And we who have the first fruits,
are groaning also inwardly.
Why is life often infused,
with so many thorns among the roses?
How can I have such deep joy,
while sad carries the sting it imposes?
Enjoying unhindered belly laughs,
soaking in good humor until I cry.
No sooner does happiness surround me,
then deep sadness completes my sigh.
A lullaby gently chiming,
as a new baby has been born.
A sad song musing in my mind,
when from a loved one I am torn.
The sweet voices of my children,
so removed from deep patterns of hate.
The clamor of bitter adults,
and the anger they seem to create.
The beauty of a lasting marriage,
the ugly divorce that forces its end.
The loyal company of a kindred spirit,
the harsh betrayal of a dear friend.
A loving embrace from one I trust,
abuse from the one called to protect.
The exquisite delight of a feast,
a nauseated tummy that aches with regret.
The warm glorious sun on my skin,
and the brutal face-slap of the cold.
The gift of youth, energy, and health,
the aches and tiredness of growing old.

We're reminded of God's goodness,
a thousand times each day.
While also knowing in our hearts,
it's not supposed to be this way.
Futility, grievance, suffering,
tears and heartache brew.
But he who subjected us to this,
did so because of the hope he foreknew.
For from the fall our plight was set,
we live under Adam and are bound.
Yet Jesus Christ our Conqueror,
has come to ensure those lost be found.
He who was infinitely perfect,
became sin for us indeed.
In this great exchange we gained,
the righteousness we desperately need.
To stand before the throne of God,
forgiven, safe, and clean.
He took our guilt and shame,
making holy and pure what was obscene.
For unlike other gods of old,
he did not stand removed.
The mess we made he came to clean,
and through his obedience he proved.
That he is a God who understands,
for he experienced it all.
The misery, the frustration,
the pain we have in Adam's fall.
But unlike Christ we don't deserve,
all the goodness that we know.
The Second Adam, truly innocent,
confronted sin and became low.
He identifies with our broken world,
radiating his glory all the more.
He's the treasure we ought to behold,
and a Savior we can adore.
For from the emptiness of our table,
we look to a God who would condescend.

And bring us to his triumphant feast,
where one day all the thorns will end.
Jesus proves that God is for you,
against you none can be.
He who did not spare his only Son,
will graciously love you through eternity.
What shall separate you,
from the love of Christ so dear.
Not tribulation, distress, persecution,
famine, nakedness, danger, or fear.
We are more than conquerors,
through him who loves us so.
Not death, nor life, nor rulers,
nor any powers on earth below.
The love of God in Christ Jesus our Lord,
is making all things one day become new.
And one day all the roses of joy,
will smell sweet without hurting you.

Ponder

Consider the fact that creation (rocks, trees, birds, seas) longs to be freed from its bondage to corruption and obtain the freedom of the glory of the children of God. If God planted that longing in creation itself, how much more is it right for his children to long for that day?

Stay

What are the thorns, the pressure points, the places of futility in your life right now? How can you grow in letting these lead you to Christ and all his benefits, rather than away from him?

Pray

Romans 8:20, 24–25: "For the creation was subjected to futility, not will-ingly, but because of him who subjected it, in hope . . . for in this hope we were saved. Now hope that is seen is not hope. For who hopes for what he sees? But if we hope for what we do not see, we wait for it with patience."

Romans 8:35, 37–39: "Who shall separate us from the love of Christ? Shall tribulation, or distress, or persecution,, or famine, or nakedness, or danger, or sword? No, in all these things we are more than conquerors through him who loved us. For I am sure that neither death nor life, nor angels nor rulers, nor things present nor things to come, nor powers, nor height nor depth, nor anything else in all creation, will be able to separate us from the love of God in Christ Jesus our Lord."

38. HIS BEAUTY ON DISPLAY

Nestled in at the end of my day,
having shuffled from task to task.
Banging out projects like Chip and Jo,
yet as you put your feet up you may ask.
What exactly have I done today?
What meaning did it bring?
Did I take time with my child,
enjoy their question, hear them sing?
So often as I parent,
my children become obstacles to my goals.
In my seeking after accomplishments,
I just hop over their little souls.
Children are messy and needy,
and they often create chaos I disdain.
Undoing everything I've done,
their inopportune timing drives me insane.
Sometimes we expect a finished product,
perfection, maturity, and wisdom.
We forget they are in process,
and the deposit we can give them.
Yes, the dishes need to be loaded,
their school work needs to get done.
Yes, I have my own projects,
and I'm always needed by someone.
But have I pondered with them,
stopped to watch a sunset with our time?
Dug a little bit deeper,
to ask what's on their mind?
Parents wear many hats,
serving, feeding, and providing.
But the greatest privilege that we have,
is to teach our littles about abiding.
You must slow down to speed up,
if their hearts your main task be.
Take opportunities to disciple,
to love and shepherd consistently.

Their up and down emotions,
can help me discover the root of their angst.
Teaching them about their hearts,
is worth more than gold despite a lack of thanks.
Asking good questions,
studying them well.
What is it they're craving,
that hides itself in angry yells?
Seeing interruptions not as hindrances,
but as opportunities to lead.
Outbursts, sadness, talking back,
truly windows into their deepest need.
And as my child fumbles and falls,
ensnared by trials and missing the mark.
The greatest help that I can offer,
is the only place I know to start.
Give her Jesus in the morning,
represent Jesus every night.
Give him Jesus in the struggle,
tell him only Jesus can make it right.
Only Jesus can cleanse her from her sin,
only Jesus' blood for him can atone.
In Jesus is found all grace and mercy,
so my child will never be alone.
And when I fail and let them down,
as even the best of parents do.
I won't succumb to despair,
but instead focus on what's true.
In Jesus, washed and sanctified,
justified, my ledger is clear.
Because Jesus Christ took the wrath,
now to my God I can draw near.
He will lift me from the miry bog,
and set my feet upon the rock secure.
A new song of praise I'll forever sing,
for in Jesus the Father sees me as pure.
In his strength and by his grace,
witnessing to his glory is worth my labor today.

No moment will ever be wasted,
when I put the beauty of Christ on display.

Ponder

Consider that Jesus did his best work in people's lives not when they succeeded, but when they failed. Their sin became the occasion for his grace to become beautiful and powerful. His mission was not morality, but redemption. This is exactly how he is relating to you as your Lord, Savior, and Friend.

Stay

Where can your children's failures become less about morality and more about redemption? Where can you bring less law and more gospel? Where do they need to hear less bad news about their inability and more good news about Jesus' magnificent ability?

Pray

Zechariah 9:16: "On that day the LORD their God will save them, as the flock of his people; for like the jewels of a crown they shall shine on his land. For how great is his goodness, and how great his beauty!"

John 4:10–14: "Jesus answered her, 'If you knew the gift of God, and who it is that is saying to you, 'Give me a drink,' you would have asked him, and he would have given you living water.' The woman said to him, 'Sir, you have nothing to draw water with, and the well is deep. Where do you get that living water? Are you greater than our father Jacob? He gave us the well and drank from it himself, as did his sons and his livestock.' Jesus said to her, 'Everyone who drinks of this water will be thirsty again, but whoever drinks of the water that I will give him will never be thirsty again. The water that I will give him will become in him a spring of water welling up to eternal life.'"

Titus 3:4–7: "But when the goodness and loving kindness of God our Savior appeared, he saved us, not because of works done by us in righteousness, but according to his own mercy, by the washing of regeneration and renewal of the Holy Spirit, whom he poured out on us richly through Jesus Christ our Savior, so that being justified by his grace we might become heirs according to the hope of eternal life."

39. LET CONVICTION LEAD TO CHRIST

Do you ever sit down at the end of the day,
feeling like a wretch and a fool?
I was impatient, angry, and so forlorn,
letting my emotions just overrule.
My child's creativity stunted,
as I barked "please put that away."
"Mommy—she hit me, she's being mean."
"Please kids, I can't take it today."
How easy it is to blame their quarrels,
to feel like everything is opposing me.
I dropped my glass, I banged my elbow,
"Lord why?", comes my frustrated plea.
Why can't I get out of this funk?
Where is my joy? I need it back.
So I fight and pray and call out for help,
and the Holy Spirit begins to gain track.
What causes quarrels and fights among you?
Is it not that my passions are trying to reign?
I desire and do not have, I covet galore,
and at the root I inflict my own pain.
My kids and my husband do not cause me to sin,
nor does the spilled drink or my frustrated plan.
I do not have because I do not ask,
and deeper and deeper from God I ran.
What am I wanting? Is this all about me?
Ahhhh there is the answer, I sigh.
And I slip away to have a moment alone,
"Forgive me." "Please help me," I cry.
Help me to remember life's not about me,
surrender my will and my heart.
To God who is the lifter of my head,
and let tomorrow be a fresh start.
For I know my heart is deceitful,
so fickle, so weak, and can fail.
But I know the one who has defeated my sin,
and his righteous in me will prevail.

There is no guilt, there is no shame,
he has nailed that to the cross for me.
So when I turn away from sin,
and run to him, I see that I'm free.
Free to admit my faults and my sins,
to admit the depth of what brews inside.
But free indeed to say with joy,
he who declared, "It is finished," is on my side.
Jesus will never leave me or forsake me,
his righteousness in me will stand.
And nothing I could ever do,
will pluck me from his hand.
So I press on toward more holiness,
the upward prize of Christ alone.
And long for when all striving ceases,
as he works on me until I'm home.

Ponder

For the Christian, feeling conviction is a gift. It is an invitation to become more fully alive in Christ. An invitation to put to death the sin that makes you miserable, and to make alive the righteousness that brings joy and peace.

Stay

If Jesus is the most approachable, the most gentle, the most compassionate person in the world (and he is), what should your first instinct be when you feel conviction over sin?

Pray

Ephesians 2:4–5: "But God, being rich in mercy, because of the great love with which he loved us, even when we were dead in our trespasses, made us alive together with Christ . . . "

1 Peter 2:10: "Once you were not a people, but now you are God's people; once you had not received mercy, but now you have received mercy."

1 Peter 3:18: "For Christ also suffered once for sins, the righteous for the unrighteous, that he might bring us to God, being put to death in the flesh but made alive in the spirit . . . "

40. HOPE IN AN EVIL AGE

So many questions,
my heart has wrestled to know.
Why it seems that evil wins,
and feels lately the status quo.
I long to see true goodness come,
for all to be made right.
Where man can dwell in safety,
and dawn replace the night.
But this is still a fallen world,
since the apple first we ate.
Love of self, our default,
and God who we do hate.
Evil is confounding,
poses questions we desire to know.
But the biggest evil that I face,
is an unlikely closer foe.
If I'm honest with myself,
my own heart is a cesspool of grievous sin.
And so in attempting to understand,
my hope is not found within.
Rather let my refuge be,
to look outside my shell.
To where wisdom, love, peace and justice,
in one person dwell.
A God who is not far off,
but in Jesus has come near.
He took on flesh, he bore our sin,
knows our weakness and our fear.
Jesus, who walked through chaos and sin,
and yet he never fell.
But pressed on steadfast to obey,
despite attacks of evil he knew well.
Bringing peace to creation,
calming waves and saving souls.
Now ruling over the universe,
my fearful heart he can console.

So when I read the paper next,
and my stomach tightens in a ball.
I pray my God will hold me up,
and grant me faith lest I should fall.
I'll pray for those who are wayward, sad,
need help and to belong.
I'll press on in what God's called me to,
and work while I sing this prayerful song:

Lord help me to have abundant life,
spiritual strength as I run this race.
Towards Jesus, my one true home,
him I long to soon embrace.
Help me do the work you've given,
encourage a friend in need and pray.
Be uncomfortable serving others,
they need my good works today.
Love my spouse, cherish my kids,
rejoice and not complain.
Because the love that I've received,
is greater than any earthly gain.
For some things are too high for me,
but faithful I must be.
With all the days he's given,
as I trust in Christ, my victory.

Ponder

Christianity promises that, in the end, good will triumph over evil. Meditate
on why that is really good news for our souls, our bodies, and our world.

Stay

Confess to the Lord the specific manifestations of evil that bother you most.
Lament them and petition the Lord to act according to his promises.

Pray

Psalm 131:1–2: "O LORD, my heart is not lifted up; my eyes are not raised too high; I do not occupy myself with things too great and too marvelous for me. But I have calmed and quieted my soul, like a weaned child with its mother; like a weaned child is my soul within me . . . "

Psalm 56:3–4: "When I am afraid, I put my trust in you. In God, whose word I praise, in God I trust; I shall not be afraid. What can flesh do to me?"

Romans 8:19–23: "For the creation waits with eager longing for the revealing of the sons of God. For the creation was subjected to futility, not willingly, but because of him who subjected it, in hope that the creation itself will be set free from its bondage to corruption and obtain the freedom of the glory of the children of God. For we know that the whole creation has been groaning together in the pains of childbirth until now. And not only the creation, but we ourselves, who have the firstfruits of the Spirit, groan inwardly as we wait eagerly for adoption as sons, the redemption of our bodies."

41. NO DEPTH WITHOUT DIFFICULTY

Friendships that are smooth,
are a gift we work to find.
The ones that come with ease,
have first stood the test of time.
For surely every relationship,
will hit a bumpy road.
A conflict comes, a fight ensues,
the newness becomes old.
It's inevitable for turmoil,
and friendship to coincide.
When two people become friends,
the sin just cannot hide.
A comment, an action, an attitude,
a quirk, a distasteful slight.
A cold shoulder, an ignoring,
or an all-out heated fight.

Wherever on the spectrum,
all friendships wander to this place.
In those moments we have a choice,
to get sour or to give grace.
Let's love instead of growing angry,
and confront our friend in such a way.
That brings forth peace and gives no room,
for Satan's evil work to play.
If we are bound up in Jesus Christ,
and for our sin he has atoned.
Then now we walk by the Spirit,
and in these battles are not alone.
Let not the sun go down on anger,
or worse the bitterness set in.
Instead we go to the person we love,
and confess to them our sin.
For we know seething has no point,
nor on their faults getting obsessed.
For even in the toughest quarrels,

we need to see in them the best.
For whatever is lovely, whatever is pure,
whatever is noble and true.
These are the things our Father in Heaven,
has chosen to see in me and you.
We are hidden in his Son,
and our sin is not held against us anymore.
So how can we hold it against another,
and not desire to have our hearts restored?
It's in these moments the Spirit helps us,
to abound with love to God and man.
Even in those relationship troubles,
we don't fully understand.
He promises to be with us,
as we walk by faith in his grace.
Seeking to imperfectly love another,
and continue to run the race.
And sometimes after a trial,
a friendship with ups and downs.
He is kind to surprise and delight us,
for a deeper friendship has been found.

Ponder

Jesus tells his disciples that he no longer considers them servants, but his friends (John 15:15). They know that because he reveals everything the Father has told him. Ponder the amazing truth that the whole Bible is Jesus confiding in you as a friend. It is revelation from the Father, in the Son, by the Spirit. It is him sharing all the riches of wisdom and knowledge with those he is closest to.

Stay

Think about your closest friends. How did God use conflict, tension, and adversity to deepen your relationship? Let his faithfulness in the past help you trust him in the present and the future.

Pray

Proverbs 27:6: "Faithful are the wounds of a friend; profuse are the kisses of an enemy."

Psalm 25:14: "The friendship of the LORD is for those who fear him, and he makes known to them his covenant."

John 15:11–15: "These things I have spoken to you, that my joy may be in you, and that your joy may be full. "This is my commandment, that you love one another as I have loved you. Greater love has no one than this, that someone lay down his life for his friends. You are my friends if you do what I command you. No longer do I call you servants, for the servant does not know what his master is doing; but I have called you friends, for all that I have heard from my Father I have made known to you."

42. CONFESSIONS OF A SEQUESTERED SPOUSE

Have I looked right past you,
as strangers passing in the night?
Have we become great roommates,
and forgotten our delight?
Remember when our hearts beat fast,
anticipating time together again?
Remember when we stayed up late,
wishing the night would never end?
I loved your smile, I loved your laugh,
the way you used to look at me.
I loved the affections of being young,
and all the rush, and fun, and glee.
Here you are still with me,
if the Lord has deemed it so.
And yet sometimes I do forget,
look past you and on I go.
The children get my attention,
I ask them questions all the time.
But have I forgotten my old love,
the one who used to occupy my mind?
Have I asked you a question today?
Have I sought to understand your soul?
Or have I fussed over countless tasks,
the mess to clean, ambition my goal.
Your clothes I used to put to my face,
because they smelled a bit like you.
And how I loved your quirks and traits,
that made me stay a moment or two.
Now I complain of your shoes by the door,
and the mess that you leave around.
I forget that you are human and weak,
and no one with perfect habits is to be found.
I snuggled with our children today,
I kissed them when they were hurt.
But when you shared your difficult day,
everything I said was unkind and curt.

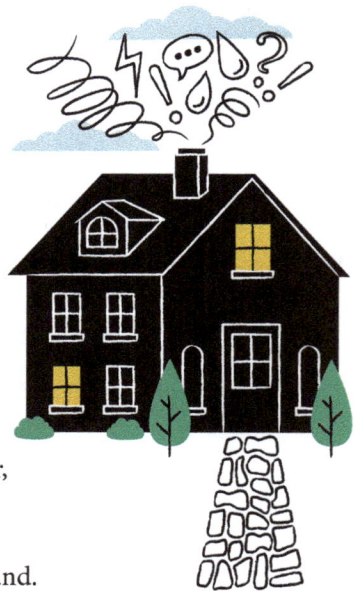

I forgot to gently touch you today,
to rub your shoulders and hold your hand.
To remember you have struggles,
and to seek to understand.
I prioritized my favorite hobbies,
my comfort, my friends, my rest.
But today I forgot God gave you to me,
and to you I should give my best.
You are my closest friend,
and you've chosen to set me apart.
Denying all others who have come,
committing to me with all your heart.
Enjoyment can be found again,
choosing to love you when it's tough.
For God looked at my lowly estate,
and moved towards me when I was rough.
The vows are what keep us,
not feelings that come and leave.
A performance-driven marriage,
can easily slip in and deceive.
God does not demand from me,
the things I so often demand from you.
Waiting impatiently for me to change,
tapping his toe as my failures ensue.
Oh how patient he is with me,
when I continue to pierce his side.
Living for my selfish desires,
indulging my flesh then running to hide.
Instead he looks upon my lowly estate,
where redemptive love has brought me in.
As he sees my heart he sees his Son,
who has taken the penalty and guilt for my sin.
Our spouse can never fully satisfy,
every desire we have inside.
Only Jesus can carry that weight,
and only in him can we overcome pride.
And he who has brought you together,
no man can ever separate.

Marriage is meant to reflect our Christ,
and the church he died to create.
God will never leave us or forsake us,
his precious blood has declared it so.
He is fully committed to us,
his grace in our marriages we can bestow.
Play together, make time to laugh,
serve without wanting a better return.
Put on patience, forgive more quickly,
don't let anger and frustrations burn.
Address the problems, not ignore,
don't sweep them under the rug.
This requires some conversation,
so it may look like wisdom to unplug.
See the good in our spouse,
the person God desires them to be.
Be part of what he is working in them,
they need our help so that they can see.
What would serve our spouse?
how can we show Christ's love today?
By the Spirit's strength and not our own,
Lord sustain our marriages please I pray.

Ponder

Think on how Jesus always made the right decision in how he used his time, in the words he spoke, in the choice to be alone or with others. Remind yourself that his perfection is now yours, by grace through faith.

Stay

Thank God for one specific quality in your spouse that has enriched your life and shown you Jesus. Then share it with them as an encouragement.

Pray

John 13:14: "If I then, your Lord and Teacher, have washed your feet, you also ought to wash one another's feet."

Hebrews 13:4: "Let marriage be held in honor among all . . . "

1 John 3:16: "By this we know love, that he laid down his life for us, and we ought to lay down our lives for the brothers."

43. HE GIVES, HE TAKES AWAY

Blessed be our God,
of all kingdoms and all might.
Who gives and takes away,
and determines for us our plight.
He gives wisdom to the wise,
and knowledge to those who seek.
He gives strength to the faint,
he upholds those who are weak.
He gives rains on the earth,
and sends water on the fields.
He gives snow like wool,
and the frost he may but yield.
He gives the beasts their food,
and young ravens that cry.
He determines the number of stars,
and gives their names in the sky.
He gives you your birthplace,
your parents, your sister, your brother.
He determines your allotted places,
your boundaries like no other.
He gives you your frame,
your inward parts knit together.
In his book all your days,
were written down from forever.
He gives you your features,
he's made you just right.
He gives you the family,
that brings hurt or delight.
He gives you gifts,
he does not give you them all.
He gives you opportunity,
or allows you to stumble and fall.
He gives you friendships,
he takes friends away.
He gives you deep trials,
while joy melts into dismay.

He gives you that job,
he gives you that rejection.
He keeps you from success,
knowing it's for your protection.
He gives you the health you want,
he strips health from your hand.
He gives you a spouse,
he takes away your marriage plan.
He gives you a baby boy,
when you have prayed for a girl.
He closes your womb,
your mind is in a whirl.
He gives you belly laughs,
and memories so precious and sweet.
He gives you the sting,
of a life still incomplete.
Sometimes, "Where are you Lord?"
"Have you left the throne on which you reign?"
Other days, "You are so good, Lord Jesus
I am thankful for so much, in your name."
But in all that he gives,
and all he takes away.
His character is never changed,
an immutable God on display.
For who has known the mind of God,
or who has counseled one so great?
Who is greater than their Savior,
to not endure both love and hate?
God's love is of a different kind,
it's depth beyond what we can conceive.
Though he does not enjoy affliction,
heartache is sent to help you believe.
For if you let him break through,
you'll become who you're meant to be.
As he chisels and purifies,
it is Christ-likeness forming incrementally.
You can rejoice and be glad in him,
for his steadfast love is near.

In the valley he is nearest,
preserving his beloved through their tears.
For those who trust in the blood of Christ,
nothing given or taken disrupts his will.
A quiet heart accepts with peace,
the story the Author writes with his quill.
The Lord will never forsake his people,
preserved forever are the children of God.
Even though the hand we're dealt
can feel so perplexing and odd.
So we can say, "Blessed be the name of the Lord,"
his great mercy has given us hope.
Through the resurrection of Jesus Christ,
we gain the inheritance of which he spoke.
Imperishable, undefiled,
unfading, kept in heaven for you.
Protected by the power of God,
through faith for a salvation glorious and true.

Ponder

Read Job chapter 1. Think on the magnitude of Job's statement in 1:21 and God's clarifying comment in 1:22.

Stay

What have been the greatest gifts God has given you? What have been the most crushing things he has taken away? How does the unchanging act of Jesus' death and resurrection free you to bless God's name no matter what happens?

Pray

Job 42:1–6: "Then Job answered the LORD and said: "I know that you can do all things, and that no purpose of yours can be thwarted. 'Who is this that hides counsel without knowledge?' Therefore I have uttered what I did not understand, things too wonderful for me, which I did not know. 'Hear, and I will speak; I will question you, and you make it known to me.' I had heard of you by the hearing of the ear, but now my eye sees you; therefore I despise myself, and repent in dust and ashes."

Psalm 147:3-5: "He heals the brokenhearted and binds up their wounds. He determines the number of the stars; he gives to all of them their names. Great is our Lord, and abundant in power; his understanding is beyond measure."

Matthew 26:39: "And going a little farther he fell on his face and prayed, saying, 'My Father, if it be possible, let this cup pass from me; nevertheless, not as I will, but as you will.'"

44. RENEW YOUR MIND

What are you putting in your mind?
Today what are you looking for?
Do you need to put down your phone,
and let your mind rest on something more?
Guard your mind from fretting,
perhaps stewing on something you read.
Refreshing, scrolling, looking again,
and letting all the bad news fill up your head.
Stay informed, yes,
use social media sparingly.
But encourage friends through it,
then log off and be free.
Go outside and watch the birds,
tickle your child and play.
Write a card, Skype someone,
call that person you've put on delay.
Build a fort, read out loud,
watch a good movie snuggled up with tea.
And when you catch your mind amiss,
ask the Lord for grace to help you flee.
Replace our fear with specific truth,
our unbelief with trust and peace.
A pure heart, a good conscience,
and a sincere faith that would increase.
Seeking to understand my friend,
before I let the sun go down on my rage.
Charitably relating always,
to all of those with whom I engage.
The lips of the wise spread knowledge,
and a gentle tongue is a tree of life.
A glad heart makes a cheerful face,
and a man of understanding brings God delight.
For the plans of the heart belong to man,
but the answer of the tongue from the Lord will arise.
As we commit our minds to him,
our walk is transformed and we'll become wise.

Lord help us to redeem this time,
think on what is beautiful, lovely and true.
For the days are evil but Jesus has come,
And he's coming again to make all things new.

Ponder

Faith in God results in a quiet mind. Consider that God's heart is for you to completely let go of the vast majority of what you worry about.

Stay

What activities help your mind focus on the good, the true, and the beautiful? What activities prompt your mind to focus on the negative, the worldly, and the digital? Ask for God's power to help change habits that need changing.

Pray

Isaiah 26:3: "You keep him in perfect peace whose mind is stayed on you, because he trusts you."

Romans 12:2: "Do not be conformed to this world, but be transformed by the renewal of your mind, that by testing you may discern what is the will of God, what is good and acceptable and perfect."

Colossians 3:2–3: "Set your minds on things that are above, not on things that are on earth. For you have died, and your life is hidden with Christ in God."

45. A HARD WEEK

Are you having a hard week,
impatient, tired, weighed down?
Working hard to seek for joy,
is there any out there to be found?
This fight is all too common,
in these human bodies that we dwell.
My emotions rolling over,
and my heart begins to swell.
Self-focus starts to rear,
its ugly head into my days.
Lying voices creep in,
and add to all the haze.
What am I supposed to do with this,
Try harder? Run away?
No, the Spirit whispers,
embrace the week and stay.
Turn away from self,
listen to God and pray.
Cry out for his mercies,
each morning, all the day.
When my heart is overwhelmed;
lead me to the rock that is higher than I.
Give me grace to know your love,
and trust in the one who hears my cries.
Early I will seek you,
get my body out of bed.
My lips shall praise you all the day,
for you are the lifter of my head.
If the Son has set me free,
than I am free indeed.
The throne of grace accessible,
where my Savior lives to intercede.
He knows my weakness and my sin,
he is substituting good fruit in their place.
Giving me his righteousness,
taking to the cross all my disgrace.

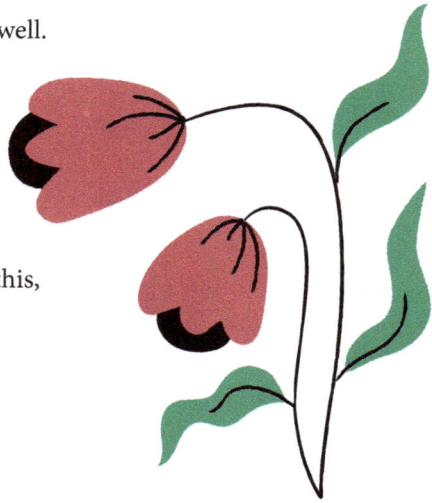

Vindicated when he rose again,
sitting down at the Father's right hand.
So my hard weeks are not lost on him,
they are something he fully understands.
When from a place of rest in Jesus,
I serve with the same love that I've been shown.
And fight for joy by his Spirit,
I can know I'm never walking alone.
Blessed is the man whose hope IS the Lord,
he will not be anxious in a week of drought.
For his roots will be deep in the river,
and the fruit from his branches will sprout.
Rejoice always, pray without ceasing,
be thankful in all he has done.
Remember although the battle feels heavy,
in the end victory has already been won.

Ponder

The Bible has the perfect balance of, on the one hand, honestly lamenting sin and suffering, not diminishing their reality. On the other hand, the Bible doesn't fixate on the bad things because of the hope found in God and the gospel. How does that balance lead to a life of stability and rest?

Stay

Both trials and victories can be temptations toward self-absorption. For you personally, how can a hard week turn you inward ("Me, me, me") rather than outward ("God, others")?

Pray

Psalm 61:1–2: "Hear my cry, O God, listen to my prayer; from the end of the earth I call to you when my heart is faint. Lead me to the rock that is higher than I . . . "

Jeremiah 17:7–8: "Blessed is the man who trusts in the LORD, whose trust is the LORD. He is like a tree planted by water, that sends out its roots by the stream, and does not fear when heat comes, for its leaves remain green, and is not anxious in the year of drought, for it does not cease to bear fruit."

Colossians 1:23: ". . . continue in the faith, stable and steadfast, not shifting from the hope of the gospel that you heard . . ."

46. WISDOM V. FOLLY

In an age of information,
too much for our minds to bear.
Misleading headlines, depressing news,
now so much more aware.
We're suddenly all experts,
because we read an article or two.
And so we get fired up,
angry judgments start to brew.
Or perhaps we turn to fear,
grasping to control our world so tight.
Our viewpoint becomes gospel,
as we try to get it all just right.
We yearn for leaders with integrity,
for clarity and truth to be widespread.
And we forget God sometimes call us,
to walk in gray areas instead.
Our world is starved for wisdom,
a godly virtue, a lost art.
Yet in a world of constant voices,
this is the place we need to start.
Wisdom builds her house,
has set her table to bring life.
Whereas folly is loud and seductive,
sits at her door and causes strife.
Wisdom offers delicious bread,
and finer wine to drink.
Folly calls much louder,
makes you react rather than think.
Wisdom takes instruction,
and seeks to understand.
Folly is pride's brother,
and likes to hear itself grandstand.
Wisdom will make you humble,
and flourish like a green leaf.
Folly is without discretion,
just as a foolish son brings his parents grief.

Wisdom builds her house,
and fears the Lord in the way she ought.
Folly believes everything she hears,
and follows the crowd without a thought.
Wisdom doesn't vent its spirit,
but is wise and gentle with her lips.
Folly feeds on foolish words,
and bitterness makes her slip.
Wisdom considers biblical categories,
the glory of kings is to search things out.
Folly trusts her own mind,
and let's emotions reduce her clout.
Wisdom is marked by honor,
but knows humility must come first.
Folly gives a quick answer,
before she hears she wants to burst.
Who can hold such wisdom?
Who can be a faithful one?
Who can say I made myself pure?
Only Jesus Christ the Son.
Who destroys the wisdom of the wise,
and the discernment of discerning thwart?
Christ crucified, the power of God,
in the halls of wisdom he holds court.
If any of you lacks wisdom,
ask God for he generously will give.
Pure, peaceable, and gentle,
open to reason so that you may live.
Full of mercy and good fruits,
impartial, sincere, as you run the race.
Look to Christ where hidden treasures,
are wisdom, knowledge, and grace.
And as you struggle with the tension,
of wanting all to be black and white.
Remember a harvest of righteousness,
is sown when we hold to wisdom tight.
The wisdom from above,
can only be well applied.

When we've received it from the Lord,
and in his word and love abide.
Ask him to show you where,
you must incline your heart to hear.
For if you search for it as hidden treasure,
the wisdom of God will truly appear.

Ponder

How does a Christian who reads their Bible but not the newspaper become
unbalanced and ineffective? What about one who reads only the newspaper
and not their Bible? Why is the Bible always primary?

Stay

What is one area of wisdom and discernment you'd like to grow in? Some
examples in Proverbs would include: expressing emotions; speaking and
listening; business ethics; family relationships; fights and conflicts; making
decisions; work; parenting; and money. Make list of Scriptures that relate to
your chosen topic, begin to memorize them, and ask the Lord for the gift
of wisdom.

Pray

Psalm 2:1–12: "Why do the nations rage and the peoples plot in vain? The
kings of the earth set themselves, and the rulers take counsel together,
against the LORD and against his Anointed, saying, 'Let us burst their
bonds apart and cast away their cords from us.' He who sits in the heavens
laughs; the Lord holds them in derision. Then he will speak to them in his
wrath, and terrify them in his fury, saying, 'As for me, I have set my King on
Zion, my holy hill.' I will tell of the decree: The LORD said to me, 'You are
my Son; today I have begotten you. Ask of me, and I will make the nations
your heritage, and the ends of the earth your possession. You shall break
them with a rod of iron and dash them in pieces like a potter's vessel.' Now
therefore, O kings, be wise; be warned, O rulers of the earth. Serve the

LORD with fear, and rejoice with trembling. Kiss the Son, lest he be angry, and you perish in the way, for his wrath is quickly kindled. Blessed are all who take refuge in him.

Proverbs 2:6–8: "For the LORD gives wisdom; from his mouth come knowledge and understanding; he stores up sound wisdom for the upright; he is a shield to those who walk in integrity, guarding the paths of justice and watching over the way of his saints."

Colossians 2:2–3: ". . . to reach all the riches of full assurance of understanding and the knowledge of God's mystery, which is Christ, in whom are hidden all the treasures of wisdom and knowledge."

47. HELLO DARKNESS, MY OLD FRIEND

The days are pressing on oh Lord,
and the grooves are setting in.
A new normal is in place it seems,
and it is grinding me down so thin.
I have too many unresolved questions,
and how to move forward is my unknown.
As a deep longing presses on my heart;
the feeling more and more of being alone.
Extrovert, or Introvert doesn't matter,
I am wired for fellowship with another.
Somehow I've entered this loneliness,
and I long for my sister and my brother.
Lately I feel the Psalmist's words,
my companions stand aloof from my plague.
My nearest kin stand far off,
and all the reasons for it feel so vague.
I'm seeking ways to combat loneliness,
in all areas of my life as I let you lead.
But oh Lord it's so hard to endure,
when it seems this loneliness will never leave.
So as I fight this fight of despair,
and attempt to give my heart to the time at hand.
Let it remind me what you created me for,
though this is not something I would've planned.
Fellowship, companionship, laughter,
touch, affection, embrace.
Nearness, conversation, relationship,
I need side by side and face to face.
You are not indifferent God,
to these desires I have inside.
Father, Son, and Spirit,
deep relationships in the Trinity reside.
Perfect friendship and pure enjoyment,
fellowship in eternity before time.
Thank you Jesus that you came,
so a taste of that enjoyment could be mine.

For though my iniquities have overtaken me,
and are more than the hairs on my head.
I was washed according to your mercy,
and now I exult in you God instead.
The friendship of the Lord is for those who fear him,
I cry out to him when no one else hears.
And through my loneliness Jesus you're near me,
you hold my head up and bottle my tears.
Through the wounds of Jesus I am healed,
pouring out his soul onto death in my stead.
My Savior, well acquainted with loneliness,
the Son of Man nowhere to lay his head.
Weeping may tarry for the night,
but joy comes with the morning sun.
I will be still before the Lord and wait patiently,
for one day my loneliness will be done.
I'll join in perfect fellowship,
with all the saints around your table.
In the meantime, Lord draw near to me,
I know you are willing, and you are able.

Ponder

Think of some specific ways Jesus experienced darkness and loneliness during his earthly life. How does that encourage you?

Stay

Think of one person who might be lonely and creatively reach out to them this week. How can you serve and bless them?

Pray

Isaiah 53:3–4: "He was despised and rejected by men, a man of sorrows and acquainted with grief; and as one from whom men hide their faces he was despised, and we esteemed him not. Surely he has borne our griefs and carried our sorrows . . . "

Psalm 102:7: "I lie awake; I am like a lonely sparrow on the housetop."

2 Corinthians 4:8–10: "We are afflicted in every way, but not crushed; perplexed, but not driven to despair; persecuted, but not forsaken; struck down, but not destroyed; always carrying around in the body the death of Jesus, so that the life of Jesus may also be manifested in our bodies."

48. HE IS COMING

Mourn as though you are not mourning,
this world is passing away.
Rejoice as though you are not rejoicing,
on the horizon looms a better day.
Buy and sell as though you have nothing,
anxiety, the Lord wants you to have none.
Live in light of eternity,
for he is coming, the glorious Son.
My relationships, my finances,
my possessions, and my time.
Linked to an eternal perspective,
can only then be rightly aligned.
I'll enjoy, I'll be thankful,
I'll walk and stumble, I'll be undone.
But I'll always remember the time has grown short,
Jesus is coming, the Living One.

Ponder

How often do you think about the imminent return of Christ? How does his coming, bringing an everlasting new creation of peace, act as a tonic for anxiety?

Stay

What relationship (parent, spouse, child, friend, money, job) looms too large in your heart, provoking anxiety? Consider how this reveals an attachment to a world that is passing away.

Pray

Daniel 7:13–14: "I saw in the night visions, and behold, with the clouds of heaven there came one like a son of man, and he came to the Ancient of

Days and was presented before him. And to him was given dominion and glory and a kingdom, that all peoples, nations, and languages should serve him; his dominion is an everlasting dominion, which shall not pass away, and his kingdom one that shall not be destroyed."

1 Corinthians 7:29–32: "This is what I mean, brothers: the appointed time has grown very short. From now on, let those who have wives live as though they had none, and those who mourn as though they were not mourning, and those who rejoice as though they were not rejoicing, and those who buy as though they had no goods, and those who deal with the world as though they had no dealings with it. For the present form of this world is passing away. I want you to be free from anxieties."

Revelation 1:7: "Behold, he is coming with the clouds, and every eye will see him, even those who pierced him, and all tribes of the earth will wail on account of him. Even so. Amen."

49. THE GRINCH AND THE GOSPEL

As I sat down tonight,
and read to my children aloud.
An old beloved story,
is the jewel we found.
How The Grinch Stole Christmas,
I could recite it in my sleep.
But suddenly it dawned on me,
that its themes are oh so deep.
Curmudgeonly, bitter,
the Grinch's heart is calloused.
He plots and he plans,
to destroy with such malice.
Why does he hate?
Why is he bitter?
Dr. Seuss gives an answer,
in his heart, he's a sinner.
And it rings in my ears,
another place I have read.
Where we were once foolish,
disobedient and astray led.
Slaves to our passions,
slaves to our pleasures.
Passing our days,
in malice and envy forever.
The Grinch hates the Who's,
their feasting and bells ringing.
But what he hates most of all,
is the joy in their singing.
He takes all they have,
not leaving a crumb to their name.
Their possessions, their Christmas,
making them his miserly game.
All of their wealth,
security, and fun.
Is gone in one evening,
all their comfort undone.

And then the Grinch waits,
taking joy in their pain.
Waiting for their cries,
a shout, a complain.
But to his surprise,
baffled and irked.
He finds that his effort,
his schemes have not worked.
And the response of the Who's,
is a powerful scene.
For in such a loss,
the Grinch puzzles what it could mean.
Instead of bitterness,
or shaking their fist.
How dare you God!?
How dare you strip us of this!?
No, they do not despair,
act surprised or stand agape.
There is no blame on their lips,
or attempts to escape.
Though all has been taken,
from them it appears.
They rise hand in hand,
singing joy through their tears.
Singing, singing,
how can it be?
A possession much deeper,
then a Grinch's eye can see.
Afflicted, but not crushed,
perplexed, but not in despair.
Persecuted, not forsaken,
struck down, but Christ is there.
Always being given over to death,
for Jesus' sake and for his name.
So the life of Jesus can be manifested,
in our mortal flesh the same.
And the Grinch's eyes are opened,
his heart grows 3 sizes that day.

For the singing and the joy,
has put Jesus on display.
And the goodness and loving kindness,
of our God and Savior appeared.
Saving the Grinch from his hardness,
according to God's mercy so near.
And the very things he hated,
the singing and carving the roast beast.
Transformed into his joy and delight,
as selfless serving became his feast.
He loved for he was loved first,
and it was grace that drew him in.
Something deeper, something lasting,
where no robber could break in.
For neither life, nor angels,
rulers, things present nor things to come.
Height, depth, or anything in creation,
can separate us from the Son.
If all our comforts be taken,
all our loves, delights, and treasures.
No one can touch eternity,
where his love flows without measure.
Sing, sing, sing,
despite your every loss.
There are always joys to be found,
as you gaze upon his cross.
The joy of those who love him,
is baffling, attractive and unique.
And the hardest heart can soften,
if just one word Christ speaks.

Ponder

Read "How the Grinch Stole Christmas" this week. Where do you see your-self in the story? Where do you see the gospel playing out?

Stay

Grace (kindness toward those who deserve judgment) draws people toward you. Judgment pushes them away. What is one habit of moral judgment in your life God wants to replace with a heart of grace?

Pray

Ruth 1:16–18: "But Ruth said, 'Do not urge me to leave you or to return from following you. For where you go I will go, and where you lodge I will lodge. Your people shall be my people, and your God my God. Where you die I will die, and there will I be buried. May the LORD do so to me and more also if anything but death parts me from you.' And when Naomi saw that she was determined to go with her, she said no more."

Romans 5:7–8: "For one will scarcely die for a righteous person—though perhaps for a good person one would dare even to die—but God shows his love for us in that while we were still sinners, Christ died for us."

1 Timothy 1:15–16: "The saying is trustworthy and deserving of full acceptance, that Christ Jesus came into the world to save sinners, of whom I am the foremost. But I received mercy for this reason, that in me, as the foremost, Jesus Christ might display his perfect patience as an example to those who were to believe in him for eternal life."

50. THE INCARNATION

The weary world rejoices,
as a thrill of hope has come.
Jesus thank you for entering,
the mess our sin has done.
Incarnating, condescending,
entering our world of pain.
To bring us to yourself,
in you we have such great gain.
As we rejoice in your birth,
a necessary foretold event.
We long to see you on the clouds,
returning from heaven sent.
When every knee will bow,
when every tongue will confess.
That Jesus is Lord,
and eternal glory we'll finally possess.
Until the trumpet sounds,
and we see the King of Kings.
Lord keep our faith and sustain us,
let an advent of hope in our heart spring.

Ponder

Consider the truth that when God the Son assumed humanity, he burned his passport. He will be forever "found in human form." How is that an incredible expression of love?

Stay

Are there any areas of your life where you feel God doesn't or couldn't understand you? How would believing Jesus' true and full humanity draw you closer to him?

Pray

Philippians 2:8: "And being found in human form, he humbled himself by becoming obedient to the point of death, even death on a cross . . . "

John 1:14, 16: "And the Word became flesh and dwelt among us, and we have seen his glory, glory as of the only Son from the Father, full of grace and truth. For from his fullness we have all received grace upon grace."

Isaiah 53:2–4: " . . . he had no form or majesty that we should look at him, and no beauty that we should desire him. He was despised and rejected by men, a man of sorrows and acquainted with grief; and as one from whom men hide their faces he was despised, and we esteemed him not. Surely he has borne our griefs and carried our sorrows; yet we esteemed him stricken, smitten by God, and afflicted."

51. HOPE FOR THE WEARY IN WINTER

When the winter is upon us,
the skies loom gray and dark.
The noses keep on running,
and it's too cold for the park.
The sun is straining with all its might,
to creep out from behind the skies.
My children are getting stir crazy,
and the snowy weather flies.
I can fixate on the weather,
the ice that never seems to melt.
Complain of all the sickness,
and the hand that I've been dealt.
Or I can choose to embrace joy,
and turn winter on its weary head.
Bundle the kids and take a walk,
play some music and dance instead.
I can enjoy hot cocoa,
or a warm fire, shower, or bath.
Call a friend, encourage them,
watch a movie that makes us laugh.
I can take that snotty nosed child,
and snuggle them as I say "I love you."
Hug them close and kiss their cheek,
Hmm maybe just a forehead will do!
I can remember that these days are fleeting,
and they don't have to undermine me.
For I have hope in the Son of God,
he is truly all the warmth that I need.
I can recall the one who has loved me,
and redeemed me by his blood shed.
How I have been adopted into the Beloved,
and been forgiven in him instead.
Even more the same God who loves me,
is with me and near in the mundane.
He hears all my hopes, fears and triumphs,
he understands all the tears and the pain.

He is the lifter of my head,
and has written a new song for me to sing.
And ten thousand reasons to rejoice,
so in my heart it can always be spring.
For my hope is not in this life,
I am just a sojourner passing on through.
My real hope has come and is coming again,
Jesus Christ, making all things new.

Ponder

On difficult days or in difficult seasons, how has the mercy of God shown up in small and unexpected ways? Jot down a list.

Stay

Are you aware of particular kinds of days or seasons that bring you discouragement? Find at least two spiritual promises in God's word that can help you in the battle. Then, think of at least two physical disciplines that can help you in the battle (e.g. exercise, nutrition, fun, sleep).

Pray

Psalm 13:1-2, 5–6: "How long, O LORD? Will you forget me forever? How long will you hide your face from me? How long must I take counsel in my soul and have sorrow in my heart all the day? How long shall my enemy be exalted over me? But I have trusted in your steadfast love; my heart shall rejoice in your salvation. I will sing to the LORD, because he has dealt bountifully with me."

Ecclesiastes 3:12–13: "I perceived that there is nothing better for them than to be joyful and to do good as long as they live; and also that everyone should eat and drink and take pleasure in all his toil—this is God's gift to man."

Romans 8:32: "He who did not spare his own Son but gave him up for us all, how will he not also with him graciously give us all things?"

52. ON REORIENTING CHRISTMAS CHEER

Christmas season is upon us,
wrapping, meals, and friends.
Family, in-laws, stockings filled,
Woops! Cards I forgot to send.
Preparing my home for guests,
dressing up, taking pictures and baking ham.
Running around like crazy, planning,
getting impatient with my little clan.
Wrestling my children into the car seats,
quickly scrambling to the church pew.
And then it dawns on me in my flusters,
these fleshly struggles my Savior knew.
And I slow down just a little,
take a deep breath; embrace people joyfully.
My little ones are not in the way,
they are part of God reorienting me.
They may be knocking ornaments down,
not listening, or running like gazelles.
They may be sick, tired or cranky,
but what a chance to love them well.
If I need to take things off the list,
let me simplify in this way.
My heart is what God cares about,
not all the "to do's" and productive days.
Let me speak to myself,
as I keep God's Word so near.
Fill myself with his truth,
pray to him my thoughts and fears.
Let me love my children through,
the lights, presents, food and bows.
Look them in the eye and share,
the most important thing we all should know:
Before the son of God,
was lifted up to die.
He had to take on human flesh,
body and soul in a manger he did cry.

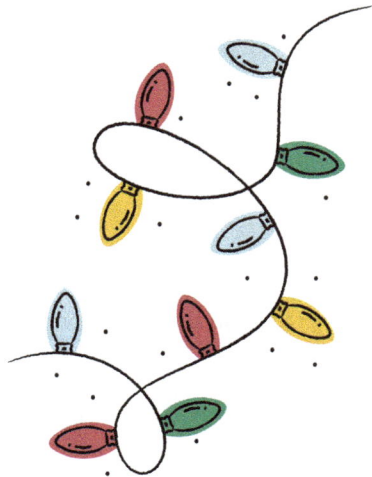

The second person of the Trinity,
left his heavenly home of bliss.
To come and save wretched sinners,
and enter a world of sin like this.
The greater prophet, priest, and king,
fulfilling the Scriptures, whom God did send.
He spoke the word, He *was* the word,
He was truth, the beginning and the end.
The priest who offered up himself,
both the offerer and the lamb.
The King who rules divinely,
yet also the servant came as man.

We love our Savior; he became like us.
We love him; he obeyed in every way.
We love him; he died a death we deserved.
We love him; he rose again the third day.
We love him; he has ascended.
We love him; he rules at God's right hand.
We love him; he will come again
We love him; and before him we shall stand.

Ponder

Meditate on how Jesus' coming has brought rest and peace to your life
where there was once exhaustion and frustration. Spiritually, emotionally,
financially, physically, and in relationships.

Stay

How much of your Christmas activity is life-giving and how much is ex-
hausting? Where can you trust God and make changes that cultivate wor-
ship over weariness?

Pray

Isaiah 54:10: "Though the mountains be shaken and the hills be removed, yet my unfailing love for you will not be shaken nor my covenant of peace be removed," says the LORD, who has compassion on you." (NIV)

Luke 2:10–11: "And the angel said to them, 'Fear not, for behold, I bring you good news of great joy that will be for all the people. For unto you is born this day int he city of David a Savior, who is Christ the Lord."

John 14:27: "Peace I leave with you; my peace I give to you. Not as the world gives do I give to you. Let not your hearts be troubled, neither let them be afraid."

Scripture Index

SCRIPTURE INDEX

Scripture Index

www.ingramcontent.com/pod-product-compliance
Lightning Source LLC
Chambersburg PA
CBHW060317100426
42812CB00003B/809